THE WONDERS

THE DEFINING STATEMENTS OF EXISTENCE

RÉNÉ GAUDETTE and MAGGIE MCGUFFIN-GAUDETTE

Edited by Lee Anne Nicholson

LIGHT Technology PUBLISHING

Edited by
Lee Anne Nicholson
Ashley E. Costanzo
Laura Monroe

ISBN 1-891824-31-7
Published by

Light Technology Publishing
P.O. Box 3540
Flagstaff, AZ 86003
1-800-450-0985
e-mail: sedonajo@sedonajo.com
www.lighttechnology.com

Printed by

Sedona Color Graphics
PRINTING SPECIALISTS
2020 Contractors Road
Sedona, AZ 86336

To Our Readers

This is the first book in a series of books to be published in which The Wonders help us to achieve empowerment.

Future volumes will cover several themes, including:

* Insights into the Workings of the Universe

* Insights to Expand Human Consciousness

* Tools to Expand Human Consciousness

This book is the first volume of the series "Insights to Expand Human Consciousness."

Love, light and peace

Réné and Maggie

Acknowledgments

This book would not have been possible without the tremendous contributions of key people in our journey.

Firstly, of course, we must thank The Wonders for having chosen us to be their messengers in this time.

Also, a great big thanks goes to our editor, Lee Anne, whose vision and courage to remain true to the words and sense of The Wonders have allowed us to produce a quality manuscript for all of our readers.

Next we must not forget our special friend and supporter, Daniel, whose desire to study with The Wonders and his willingness to choose to put into practice his learnings have brought him forward into our lives.

Also, we wish to thank all of the participants of our study groups, which formed the basis of this book, for their questions, curiosity and willingness to explore new territory.

Last but not least, we wish to express our gratitude to Light Technology Publishing, our publisher, and especially O'Ryin, who was willing to help spread the message of The Wonders.

To all those we could mention, or those we might have forgotten . . .

Love, light and peace

Réné and Maggie

Contents

Introduction

The Wonders are a collective energy consciousness channeled by deep-trance psychic Réné Gaudette. For the purpose of our understanding, they describe themselves as a group of entities numbering between three and four thousand and residing on the twenty-ninth dimension of reality, where all reality is viewed as comprising thirty-two dimensions with God/Goddess/The All That Is residing on the thirty-second dimension. They have chosen to speak at this time in order to guide individuals on their spiritual journey toward self-empowerment. Their messages are clear, easy to understand, loving, expansive, powerful and profound.

Since they know themselves to be unlimited beings, The Wonders are able to provide answers to all questions. As they provide suggestions to individuals asking questions, The Wonders expand the individual's knowledge and awareness of his or her own talents and abilities, leading him/her to greater opportunities for choice, while in no way affecting free choice and free will. In fact, this is The Wonder's only caveat: They will not interfere with an individual's free will and free choice.

This book has been developed from a series of six sessions with The Wonders on what they term "The Defining Statements of Existence." Together, these six statements define the totality of all existence throughout every dimension of reality and are intended to provide us with an opportunity for growth and understanding. As defining statements, they form the basis for this and all subsequent sessions with The Wonders. The additional comments appearing at the end of each chapter are the result of question and answer sessions held with study group participants.

In 2001, The Wonders will expand on these statements in a series of six workshops, one on each of the defining statements.

To find out more about The Wonders and how to contact us, please visit our Web site at www.thewonders.com.

CHAPTER ONE

Existence Is But an Extension of Yourself

The First Defining Statement

Upon incarnation, through the creation of ego-personality, individuals often view their existence as being limited to that which they perceive. They see themselves as being born of parents, of living an existence whereby they grow, go to school, get married, have children, have grandchildren and eventually, cast off feet of clay. They find themselves in circumstances and situations whereby, from their perspective, the totality of their existence is limited to whatever they've experienced throughout that particular portion of their existence. They see themselves as limited beings affected by circumstances, thus finding themselves reacting and responding to situations in their existence.

How many times have individuals found themselves in a certain set of circumstances whereby, from their perspective, destiny has played a part in their existence? They were destined to be at a certain point, at a certain time, to meet a certain person. As a result, they find themselves caught up with the aspect of destiny. Individuals–specifically those who, from one perspective or another, view themselves as being needy or requiring certain fulfillment in their existence–find themselves looking around for certain circumstances or situations that will complete the fulfillment of their existence.

When they find this particular complete fulfillment, they look beyond themselves to destiny, to God/Goddess/The All That Is, or to anything as being that which completes that which they are. And as a result, they see themselves as being "less than" in their existence.

You are the creators of your own "destiny"–the creators of your existence. And as a result, the circumstances or situations that you find yourselves in are, in effect, created by you–attracted by your selves to your selves in order to bring about for your selves an awareness of the expansion of your existence.

We are often asked, "What is the purpose of our existence?" And we always answer, "The purpose of your existence is to experience the experience of existence."

From that perspective, the "experience of the experience of existence" is both literally and factually to recognize and view yourselves in each moment to the completeness of that which you are. Not the partiality, but to the completeness of that which you are.

That being said, the purpose of this particular statement—"Existence Is But an Extension of Yourself"—is to allow you to recognize that you yourselves extend yourselves outward so sufficiently that you create, whether it be from the perspective of creating initially or from the perspective of attracting something to yourselves. You create incidences, circumstances or situations whereby you are presented with opportunities to choose to manifest that which you are in your completeness—all of your talents, all of your abilities. You have that opportunity in every moment of your existence. However, if you allow yourselves to manifest only a portion of your talents and abilities, then your reality will be reflected in kind. The decisions and choices you make that affect your existence—the decision or choice to react or respond to circumstances or situations, or for that matter, even to create circumstances and situations in the first place—those decisions will be based on a limited perception of that which you are. And therefore, based on this limited perception, you will find yourselves in an event, reality or existence that is limiting in and of itself.

We often speak to individuals from the perspective of belief structures. Allow yourselves to explore your belief structures sufficiently so as to recognize their limits. For each one of those belief structures, having certain limits built-in, will in effect alter and shift your reality sufficiently, creating a limited perspective of existence.

Now, recognize the word *perspective* here. This is not to say that your existence is limited. Far from it. But that with which you choose to interact within your existence is limited by the perspective of that which you yourself perceive yourself to be. And as a result, your existence becomes limited.

Now, this particular subject has much to explore. And we would urge each and every one of you to explore that which is within yourself that limits you from the exploration of that which is within yourself. Interesting comment, isn't it?

Recognize that, within yourselves, you have the talents and abilities to manifest yourselves in your completeness and in your totality. Now, what does that mean, "completeness and totality"?

As ego-personalities created by your soul-essences when you incarnated into this particular existence, you chose to incarnate based on certain parameters of existence. You chose your talents; you chose your abilities; you chose your circumstances; and you chose talents and abilities that would allow you to deal with those circumstances that you found yourselves in, that would allow you to resolve the issues of those circumstances.

As we said, you are not fools, dear friends. You have

chosen wisely in that you have chosen to manifest all that is necessary within yourselves to resolve all of the circumstances and situations in which you find yourselves in your existence.

Now, these talents and abilities, where did they come from? They came from certain aspects of yourselves, from previous experiences or existences. When an entity casts off feet of clay–as we do submit to you each time someone asks–he or she moves through the process of reintegration and reevaluation with soul-essence. This is a process whereby all choices made in existence are reviewed–not from the perspective of judgment, but rather from the perspective of how one choice led to another choice, which led to another choice, which leads to another choice. All knowledge gained from the existence is then reintegrated with soul-essence.

Therefore, when a new incarnation is created by soul-essence, all knowledge gained from all incarnations–from either previous or future incarnations, from one perspective or another–is available to the incarnation that exists. And this will lead you to other questions as well, we assure you. However, view it from this perspective: If you yourselves as incarnations have all the knowledge and all the awareness of all the incarnations of your soul-essence, then you have all the talents and abilities necessary to create an existence that resolves the issues of your existence sufficiently to create benefit.

Individuals who view themselves as simply incarnated entities, as simply being human beings, see themselves as limited by the actions of others, by the actions of their environment, by the actions of their existence. And they see themselves as having to react or respond to those actions. As a result, some grow, some learn, and some don't, moving through their existences as "best they can." And at the end of their existences, they find themselves wondering why it is that they did not accomplish that which they set out to accomplish in the beginning.

We would suggest, dear friends, that you have all the talents and all the abilities and all the awareness from all the existences in which the soul-essence has existed—sufficient to allow you to resolve all of the issues of your existence in order to move beyond the existence into a perspective of greater benefit for the totality of yourselves.

How do you tap into this knowledge and awareness? You do so by listening to yourselves. When you find yourselves in a certain circumstance whereby fear starts to manifest itself within and moves you to go from one aspect to another aspect of the self, recognize that the fear is ego-based, ego-centered. And as a result, it is based on a limited perspective of existence. Ego, after all, was created only when you incarnated, not prior, and thus sees itself as being whole and complete. Even though from one perspective, it is an extension of soul-essence, from another perspective, it does not recognize this extension of itself. As a result, it sees itself as simply being born. The beauty of the model of the ego-personality is that it is an absolute reflection of how God/Goddess/The All That Is extended itself. In effect, God/ Goddess/The All That Is extended itself by simply being. First there was one, then there was all.

The ego-personality is an extension of soul-essence. It does not recognize itself as an extension of soul-essence, however, and therefore sees itself as simply being. Upon incarnation, it thus begins to make choices that affect the existence of the soul of the incarnated entity, choices to its perceived benefit. However, its perception of benefit is limited by its knowledge and awareness of itself. When an ego-personality incarnates, it's not given a great deal of knowledge and awareness of itself. It does not perceive its talents and abilities. It does not know that which it is. And as a result, it goes through a process of learning. When the baby cries, it learns that crying results in attention, food, love and nurturing. When the child walks, it recognizes that by using certain talents and abilities, it can move, it can touch, it can feel. It can explore the senses of itself.

An ego-personality extends itself through the five senses—the ones that affect its physicality—for the ego-personality sees itself as being limited to its physicality. As an ego-personality grows and expands and becomes aware that it is more than a physicality, it attempts to incorporate within itself the awareness of its extension of itself, the awareness of an expansion of itself, based on its own perception of itself, which is limited by the five senses. Therefore, emotions are viewed through the five senses. The mental self is viewed through the five senses. And at one point in existence, the ego-personality becomes aware of itself as an extension of soul-essence and begins to manifest soul-essence in its existence.

Now, it manifested soul-essence prior to this awareness; however, it did so without the knowledge of this interconnection. And as a result, when it did, it did so based on its limited perception of itself through its five senses.

Therefore, from an ego-personality's perspective, its self-awareness is based upon its physicality, which is a limited perspective that it created by itself for itself in order to ensure its survival. Therefore, from that perspective, as the ego-personality grows and expands its perception of itself, it does so through the filters of its own physicality, of its own limitations.

And it isn't until the you that is you–that totality of your self within your self, which is the interconnection of your soul-essence to ego-personality–it isn't until that part or portion of the self begins to choose, to consciously direct the ego-personality into an expanded awareness of its interconnection to soul-essence, that the ego-personality begins to recognize the value of itself and the extension of itself. When this occurs, it then creates fear as a methodology of limiting this perception, or this expanded view, or this particular direction. For then it maintains control. It performs its function. It ensures survival through its awareness of its five senses.

And therefore, from that perspective, many individuals who embark on a journey of self-discovery, of self-expansion, often find themselves deflected, moved into different areas, moved into circumstances or situations whereby the focus becomes one of survival of the five senses—the focus of the ego-personality. And therefore, the perception remains limited. It shifts, it changes, but still, it's like a sideways step—it stays limited.

Now, when this occurs, the you that is you—the part of the self that is the interconnection of soul-essence to ego-personality—then attempts to alter and shift this perspective. Sometimes successfully, sometimes not.

As a result, existence—that which the ego-personality perceives as existence—begins to manifest itself in methodologies or paradigms that are different from its own particular perception or its own particular paradigm. Again, fear then gets created more and more and more, and limitations become imposed and accepted more and more and more.

And it isn't until the ego-personality views itself as an extension of soul-essence through the learning process, through the growth process (the same growth process it underwent from the time it was incarnated to the time it became that which it is in the moment) that the ego-personality will acknowledge itself as greater than that which it is and therefore allow the totality of the self to move to an expanded perception without fear and without limits.

From that perspective, why then do we suggest that existence is but an extension of yourselves? For from that perspective—the perspective from which we've spoken—the ego-personality, though it perceives through its five senses, does not create its existence. It simply perceives its existence and reacts to it.

Why is it then that we view existence as an extension of the self? Because from the perspective of that of which we have spoken, the ego-personality, though it views existence through its five senses in a limited fashion, is choosing through free will and free choice. It is making choices that affect its existence, the existence of itself.

A perfect example: A young child playing in a mud puddle chooses to jump into the mud puddle and get dirty. That choice will affect the remainder of that young child's existence, for when the young child comes home, if the parent chooses to discipline the child for having jumped into the mud puddle—and most often they will—then the child will react on the basis of that new awareness and learning. And therefore, the choice to explore becomes a limited choice—to explore only in certain circumstances and situations that are safe to the self.

That very small incident can affect the remainder of the existence of a person to the point that a seventy-year-old person on his deathbed, when presented with the opportunity to reconnect with soul-essence and to recognize his interconnection to all existence, may well choose not to because he fears exploration, he fears spontaneity.

Now, take another example. A young person—female, age sixteen—goes to school. During school, she has good experiences. The teachers are good, the studies are good, and she is attracted to a young man. And the young man, to a certain degree, is attracted to her. Yet the young man, for no other reason than choice, chooses to denigrate this young lady because she wears glasses. A very simple observation—this young lady wears glasses. The young man denigrates her for this, calling her "four eyes."

The young lady's particular choice to react to that particular situation—based on the ego-personality's perspective of itself as a result of the extension of its existence—can move in this fashion. If the young lady was not self-confident and perceived herself as an individual only through the awareness of others, she would take this particular comment so to heart that she would, in effect, "denigrate" her grades, lose herself in class, fail to a certain degree, even to the point of completely altering her life in the future by using contact lenses, having operations that can affect the eyes and so on.

On the other side, if the young lady had been brought up in circumstances or situations whereby she was self-actuating, self-aware, self-confident, she might well turn around and say to the young man, "Please, go take a hike." And she would say please first because she's polite.

Now, the choice of the individual affects the next choice. As we said at the beginning of this session, when an entity casts off feet of clay, choices are reviewed. When as ego-personalities, you review your existence now, in the moment, you review it through the perspective of yourselves—the perspective of your five senses, the perspective of ego-personalities. And therefore, the tendency is to review it with judgment. You review this and say, "This was good, this was bad. This was right, this was wrong." We always suggest to individuals to view their existences from the perspective of the degree of benefit.

Why do we suggest this? Because if you allow yourselves to view your existences from that perspective, you eliminate judgment—which is, in and of itself, a limiting factor. You allow yourselves to expand your perspective sufficiently to become unlimited. For there is no limit to the degree of benefit. All things have degrees of benefit; it's simply a question of which degree. As a result, existence expands. It does not contract. Once you've cast off feet of clay and moved through this process, you move through without judgment.

What is the state of *no judgment?* What is it? What does it mean to be in a state without judgment? It means to be in a state of absolute acceptance, which is the equivalent of absolute love.

Viewed from that perspective, why not therefore create for yourselves a state of absolute love without judgment, which would be a manifestation of your soul-essences' perspective? For your soul-essences are nonjudgmental, in a state of absolute love.

For the ego-personality to view itself as existing in a state of nonjudgmentalism—a state of absolute love or absolute acceptance—it would require the ego-personality not to judge itself. Yet ego-personality was created, and immediately upon creation, it judged itself. For it judged itself as being whole and complete. This was not an awareness given to it—it judged itself. It viewed itself and judged itself. And therefore, from that perspective, the ego-personality will attempt to maintain judgment in its existence, for it sees judgment as being an extension of itself.

How can existence manifest itself so sufficiently that an individual can recognize the interconnection of herself to all existence?

If you begin to view how each choice you've made in your existence has affected the next choice and the next choice and the next choice, then you will recognize how your choices have affected existence.

View it from this perspective: Today you choose to go down this road. You—all of you—came to this particular session tonight. Each of you made the choice to come to this session. And the next choice you make will be affected by this choice.

Some of you came by car. Some of you came by foot. Yet whatever choice you made affected the next choice. Some of you chose to come by foot; therefore you had to choose to take longer to get here. Some of you chose to come by car; you chose to take less time to get here. Some of you chose to come by car and took more time to get here because you didn't know where here was.

Each one has made a choice, which has led to a choice, which resulted from another choice, which resulted from another choice.

Now, let's take this forward. As you sit here and listen to our words, you are choosing–choosing to listen to certain words, to emphasize certain others, to remember and accept certain others. Each one of those methodologies will affect the next choice. They will affect the questions you ask. They will affect the remainder of your existence. For from this moment forward, each choice you make has been affected by that which you have perceived, which are the words we speak, the experience you are experiencing presently in this very moment.

Therefore, as you "experience the experience" of this particular experience, so too are you then–from one perspective–experiencing the experience of existence. For existence is simply more of these particular choices and opportunities all put together, all lumped together to create enough of a perspective to provide you with an opportunity to perceive reality from that perspective.

Why is it that you see stars in the sky? Why is it that the Moon comes up at night? Why is it that you see trees on the ground and rivers and lakes and animals and birds and insects? Why is it that you see cities and pavement, tables and chairs, cars, and a number of other things? Because you choose to perceive all of this as reality.

Your scientists would have you believe that, in effect, wood exists as it is. That, true, it is an amalgamation of atoms, but in a set function—a limited concept. Therefore, why not use that particular concept? But is wood truly a limited concept? True, from one perspective, it is an amalgamation of atoms, but are atoms themselves not energy?

And therefore, is it not the awareness, or the extension of energy, that creates? And if that is the case, then is not all existence simply energy? It is energy manifested, formed, molded into a certain methodology, a certain aspect, that fits the ego-personality's perception of its five senses. Still, it's energy.

Take the chairs you are sitting on. Each one of those has been formed by human hands using a number of materials. Yet each one of those chairs is actually energy—no more and no less—molded, formed, limited in a certain way so as to allow the ego-personality to observe existence through its five physical senses.

Is it therefore the soul-essence that has created reality? Or is it the ego-personality that has created reality? We assure you, it is both. For the ego-personality is an extension of soul-essence and as such has created its existence by manipulating energy in such a way as to satisfy its perception of itself, which is based on a limitation of the five physical senses. Once the ego-personality begins to observe itself as being more than the five physical senses, then the perception of the manipulation of energy, which is an extension of the perception of reality, alters and shifts sufficiently to allow reality to become different, to become altered, to become new.

Why is it that certain individuals can teleport themselves? Because they perceive themselves beyond the five physical senses. They are not willing to be limited by those five physical senses.

Why is it that certain individuals can make things disappear and other things appear? Because they perceive themselves as beyond their five physical senses and therefore see themselves as an extension of energy such that they allow themselves to manipulate, mold, alter and shift to the perceptions they choose. And why do others also perceive it? Because they are willing to accept another's perception of their five physical senses. If dear Maggie here had chosen to, she could move a pencil with her mind. She's tried, but hasn't yet succeeded—so she says. However, if she herself were to move that pencil with her mind, it would have to fit into the paradigm of existence that her ego-personality perceives through her five physical senses. For if she did move it beyond the five physical senses, then the fear within herself is that it would not be accepted by other ego-personalities, who would view the event. Yet, why not?

We assure you, dear friends, that if this was done by dear Maggie or any other person, it would be perceived by other ego-personalities. And it would be perceived because, from their perspective, they would see it through the perception of their five senses. They would see it through the sense of sight and the sense of sound, as well as through the other senses. They could touch it. They could smell it. If they chose to, they could taste it–though we would suggest that a pencil doesn't taste very good. However, the event itself–the occurrence of movement–would be perceived through the five senses.

Therefore, when you choose to begin moving pencils, may we suggest that you set aside the attempt to move them through an extension of your five senses that would fit the parameters of your existence as ego-personalities. Prior to this event, allow yourselves to observe yourselves as extensions of energy, as extensions of soul-essence energy. And therefore, recognize that you, dear friends, as ego-personalities, are greater than, more than, beyond the five physical senses by which your perceptions exist. Therefore, move beyond those perceptions.

The pencil is energy. It is the same energy, has the

same vibration and moves in the same fashion as you yourselves, physical human beings.

Some would argue, as a result of their own personal experiences, that a pencil surely does not have the same vibratory pattern that the human body has. And from one perspective, they would be correct. For they perceive vibration through their five physical senses.

Shift that perspective, however, to recognize that the five physical senses themselves are limiting, and then perceive the vibratory pattern from the other senses—the sixth, seventh, eighth, ninth, tenth, and so on. Then you begin to recognize that the pencil is an extension of your own energy, projected by the ego-personality and manipulated in such a fashion as to create an effect that is visible through the five physical senses.

And if the pencil is an extension of that energy, then why isn't everything else? Why is the car not an extension of your energy? Why is the tree not an extension of your energy? Why is the giraffe not an extension of your energy? Why is the horse not an extension of your energy? Why is the cat not an extension of your energy? And from one perspective, why is the person sitting next to you also not an extension of your energy?

We assure you, there is no separation between one person sitting here in this room and the person sitting next to him and the person sitting next to him. From one perspective, you all operate at the same vibratory pattern.

You have all been created as soul-essences. And from one perspective, you all are God/Goddess/The All That Is. As we said at the beginning, first there was one, then there was all.

Therefore, why isn't another individual simply an extension of your own energy? And if that individual is an extension of your energy and is, from one perspective, moving to the same vibratory pattern, why then can the choice that you make not alter that other person's existence?

Each person is an extension of soul-essence. From that perspective, it can therefore be said that each person is separate from every other person. For soul-essences, to a degree, have a certain perspective of separateness. However, as soul-essences expand their perception of themselves as individuals in existence, then so too does their perspective recognize that they are not separate existences. That rather, from one perspective, they move through to group consciousness, group existences, then to collective existences and finally to oneness, which is God/Goddess/The All That Is.

From that perspective, therefore, each entity–each physical being that you yourselves call human or non-human–is an extension of your energy. Which means that when you have chosen to do something-when you chose to jump into the puddle when you were three years old–that particular decision did not simply affect that particular child. It affected all existence around the child. It affected the water. It affected the mud. It affected the earth. It affected the insects. It affected the animals that surrounded it. It affected other people. It altered and shifted reality. For the choice to jump into the water was done through free will and free choice, and it altered reality. For, from that point on, a child had jumped in the water. That event had occurred. And therefore, from the perspective of occurrence, an altered reality exists.

Now, did the child alter her brother's reality, or her sister's? Absolutely. For when the child got home and the parent chose to discipline the child, that was also observed by other individuals, other entities. And as a result, it affected those other entities and their perceptions of choices.

Beyond the observance of the five physical senses, however, the particular awareness that discipline is the result of jumping in the water–and the choice to view that result in a fashion that would be limiting to the existence of the ego-personality known as the young child–moved through its consciousness, through the conscious and the subconscious to soul-essence, and from one perspective, was shared by all soul-essences. All existence became aware of that point in time; that moment of experience; that minute of existence; that instant of existence. All existence became aware of it instantly. (Although, from one perspective, there is no time; from your perspective, there is. Therefore, view it as instantly.)

Now, why is this? Consider that which we've just pointed out to you from the perspective of the hundredth-monkey syndrome. Why is it that one individual, in one place, can choose to perform a certain act with no other individuals being anywhere near this particular individual, yet the consciousness throughout the world is affected by it, and now, someone else does the same thing on the other side of the planet. Why is that? Because the awareness of the action permeates consciousness. It permeates existence. And therefore, all soul-essences have the ability to allow that awareness to move through to their incarnations.

It is also the ego-personality's freewill choice to listen and be aware of that awareness, of that knowledge, and apply it in its existence. Earlier, we said to each and every one of you that all that you do, all knowledge gained, is applied by soul-essence into your existence. And therefore, you have all the talents and abilities necessary to resolve the issues of your existence, to assist you to move through the experience of the existence in order to experience to the completeness and fullness the experience of your existence. This comes not simply from yourselves; it comes from all existence. For all existence is, in effect, so interrelated that when one does something, another is aware.

Most individuals do not tap into this awareness, do not allow themselves to observe themselves from the perspective of an extension of the totality of existence. Therefore, their perception is limited. It's the equivalent of seeing yourself in front of a tree. If all you can see is the tree, you think the tree is the totality of your existence.

View it from this perspective: If you were an ant and you were walking up a tree, what you would see is a large road, a rather large path for you to walk on. But now, move from the ant's perspective to a human standing in front of a tree, and you recognize that the ant's roads or paths are simply marks in the bark of a tree. Move beyond the perspective of the human to the perspective of the eagle flying above, and you recognize that the tree is simply an extension of a number of trees that form a forest. Move beyond the perception of the eagle to the perception of an astronaut circling the planet, and you recognize that the forest is simply an extension of the totality of the planet–that there are parts that are material and parts that are water. Move beyond that, and you see an extension of how this planet forms part of a solar system, which forms part of a universe, which forms part of a cosmic perspective, which forms, even beyond that, a part of the totality of all existence.

Perspective shifts and alters. If you see yourselves as simply limited ego-personalities, then you will see your existence as being simply an extension of your own particular limited perspective through the five senses of physicality.

But if you see yourselves as extensions of soul-essence, you allow yourselves to perceive existence beyond the limitations of the five physical senses. You allow yourselves to recognize how you can manipulate and mold existence in such a way as to provide you with the benefit you were seeking when you were incarnated into this existence so as to experience the experience of existence. Then you allow yourselves to change, to alter, to grow. The more you expand your perspective, the greater the opportunity for growth, the greater the opportunity for expanded effect in your existence and therefore, for an expanded existence. Limit your perception, and you limit your existence.

And from that perspective, therefore, is not the statement, "Existence Is But an Extension of Yourself," totally accurate? For the *self* describes not simply the physical self, it describes the physical, the mental, the emotional, the manifested spiritual, the ego-personality, the conscious, the subconscious, the soul-essence, the God/Goddess/The All That Is, the separateness, the group consciousness, the collective consciousness–in fact, all existence. And if you perceive it from that perspective, you then begin to recognize the abilities that exist within the self to shift and alter your existence sufficiently to create benefit to yourselves.

View it from this perspective: The person who quits school at age sixteen after having spent six years in grade seven, has a certain perspective of her existence. And everything, therefore, moves through that perspective. She sees herself as incapable, unable, unworthy, that she has a lack of ability, a lack of talent, a lack of knowledge. And therefore, existence manifests itself in kind. That person lives in subhuman surroundings, in low-income housing, and is incapable of moving, not choosing to alter or shift the reality. She sees herself as being a victim. She sees herself as being incapable. She has a child at an early age, and so forth.

Choices, choices—one choice leading to another choice, which leads to another choice. All because of perception. But if that very same person shifts the perception of herself sufficiently to recognize that the talents and abilities exist within herself to be able to extend her existence to her greater benefit, then all of a sudden, things shift. A choice is made to return to school, to extend the existence: new choices, new existences, new jobs, new clothes, new environments, new friends, new relationships, demanding more respect, demanding more of existence, demanding more of herself.

Existence changes by simply shifting one's perspective. And if existence can shift for that person, then we assure you, it has, in effect, shifted for everyone else. For all of the planet—all of the universe, in fact—has shifted because that one person has chosen to change his or her perception of himself sufficiently to recognize himself as an extension of that which he sees himself to be.

Additional Comments

On God/Goddess/The All That Is and its choice to extend itself

From one perspective, God/Goddess/The All That Is is a oneness of all existence. Recognize that. Seeing itself as a oneness of all existence, it chose to experience all facets of existence. As a result, it extended itself in order to experience all facets of existence without interference from itself. Therefore, it created free will and free choice. Free will and free choice exist throughout all aspects of existence.

From that perspective, soul-essences then also created extensions of themselves through all facets of their perception of existence, which is why, as we've suggested, there are collective consciousnesses, group consciousnesses and separate consciousnesses. Beyond that, each soul-essence, residing in a separate consciousness, also extended itself sufficiently to create aspects of existences that, from that perspective, would reflect free will and free choice. Each one of those is viewed as ego-personality–as lifetimes.

The purpose of this is simple: It's to experience the experience of existence from every facet possible. Every facet *possible*–good word–the word imaginable is limiting. Your existence is therefore an experience by your soul-essence. It is an extension. You have a number of other lives in which you also exist as well, a few coexisting at this particular moment in time. Beyond that, your soul-essence, as a singular, separate soul-essence, is also an extension of group soul-essence—a group consciousness, which, in and of itself, is also an extension of a collective consciousness, which, in and of itself, is an extension of God/Goddess/The All That Is. Therefore, all knowledge and awareness gained from this experience you call existence also affects God/Goddess/The All That Is.

From that perspective then, all other existence—all existence—is affected by your free will and your free choice in the experience of your existence. Recognize that when we use the word *affected*, we do not mean that it has a negative or a positive impact. That is a judgment that you yourselves, as ego-personalities, assign to the word. What we do mean is that there is an effect upon existence, an alteration of existence. And as a result of that alteration, existence expands.

On survival and the ego-personality

Upon incarnation, the creation of the ego-personality by the soul-essence is manifested. Viewing itself at that very instant, the ego-personality sees itself as complete and whole. However, from that perspective, it therefore also sees itself as being limited, for it recognizes its own particular perspective of limitation, that its perspective of itself is based on its own limited perspective of itself. This does not mean that the ego-personality must be limited. Rather, the soul-essence chooses to experience this portion of existence as a limited experience for the purpose of allowing itself to experience limitation.

Recognizing its own limitation, the ego-personality therefore moves to grow and expand itself from that perspective through the experience of existence. For that is its only direction from soul-essence. In effect, it is the equivalent of soul-essence saying, "Go out and experience the experience of existence." Recognizing that it must experience the experience of existence—that is its mandate—it chooses to do so in a methodology or paradigm that is sufficient for its perspective of itself. And seeing its sufficiency from that perspective, it also recognizes that it must continue to experience the experience of existence. Therefore, survival is key from the ego-personality's perspective. For without the survival of itself, it cannot experience the experience of existence. Now, as created by soul-essence, the ego-personality needs to learn. It has no awareness, no knowledge of itself beyond the awareness of itself as existing. Therefore, it experiences each experience from the perspective of its own perspective of existence.

Soul-essence has done the same. For soul-essence was created by God/Goddess/The All That Is. Soul-essence is aware of its completeness of existence. However, portions of itself are not. Therefore, as a soul-essence has extended itself from God/Goddess/The All That Is to collective consciousness, to group consciousness, to singular or separate consciousness, eventually manifesting itself as ego-personality, each of those particular aspects has a limited perspective of itself or of themselves. Their direction in existence is to reawaken to an awareness of themselves as being God/Goddess/The All That Is. Therefore, from that perspective, there is a reawakening, a relearning.

The ego-personality sees itself in a similar—although not quite the same—perspective, and therefore, the experience of ego-personality extends the awareness of itself, of soul-essence, and eventually moves and extends the awareness of soul-essence through the singular, to group, to collective, to oneness. The ego-personality does not surrender in the sense of giving up, or giving of itself. Rather, it expands itself to incorporate, to encompass the perspective of soul-essence. Which is why we often suggest that individuals view themselves as manifested spiritual entities as opposed to spiritual essences. For in effect, the ego-personality is a manifestation of spiritual essence. And from that perspective, as the ego-personality expands its perspective of itself, it recognizes its value, its interconnectedness. At that point, were the ego-personality willing to manifest itself as soul-essence, the soul-essence would allow the ego-personality to continue its existence. From the perspective of the process of reintegration and reevaluation that an entity goes through when it casts off feet of clay, what would occur is that, if the ego-personality were willing to allow itself to become soul-essence, to extend itself so completely as to manifest itself as soul-essence, at that point, ego-personality would become one with soul-essence. It would continue its existence, and consciousness would remain.

An analogy to describe the ego-personality

If you were to describe the ego-personality as a flavor—which is a good analogy; not complete, but good—then the flavor is a very complicated flavor, not a singular flavor. It has many facets. And each facet can, in and of itself, be applied by the choice of the flavor. When you describe it as a flavor, you imply direction from outside. From one perspective, the ego-personality is complete and whole, in and of itself. Therefore, it has free will and free choice. And therefore, as a flavor, it can apply itself and choose to alter itself through its own free will and free choice.

On making choices: Possibilities, probabilities and alternative realities

An awareness of choice exists. The awareness of possibilities and probabilities exist, which is why we often speak to you in terms of probabilities. It isn't that there is a creation of an alternate or parallel reality. It's simply that an awareness of choice exists. The choice to choose one probability over another is based on free will and free choice, and that choice is the result of experience. Therefore, the choice results in the experience. As to the other possibilities and probabilities not chosen, there is plenty of opportunity to experience them as well. You don't have to do it in the immediate. You perceive the choice to go left or the choice to go right. From your perception, you perceive it as being an immediate response by the universe to the particular choice. You have free will and free choice. You choose to go left, and the existence of all the universe experiences your choice to go left. Another person in the same circumstance would choose to go right, and therefore experience the choice to go right. Another time, you choose to go right instead of left. So you experience going right instead of left. At the same moment, you might choose to go left instead of right. There are so many permutations and combinations of probabilities that, we assure you, all of experience will eventually be experienced.

On when choice is made: with thought or with action?

It depends on the process–the choice to choose. The thought is a creation of choice. It is an opportunity by the ego-personality and by soul-essence to create the probability of choice. The opportunity to choose comes after thought, unless the thought is the choice itself. If the thought is the choice, then the choice comes before the thought. If the thought is the resultant of choice, then choice comes first. However, if the thought is the precursor to choice, then choice comes after.

View it from this perspective: You think. View these words. Right this very instant, thought has entered your mind. The opportunity to use that thought to create choice now approaches you. You have an opportunity. However, the opportunity to choose to think is also an opportunity. Therefore, the choice to choose to think is also a choice. Thought comes after that choice, yet it comes before the choice to do what the thought suggested, what the thought created.

On who chooses: the ego-personality or the soul-essence?

In the majority of your existences, it is the ego-personality that chooses. However, your soul can manifest itself in your existence through the free choice and free will of your ego-personality. Therefore, just as ego-personality manifests itself as soul-essence, so too does soul-essence participate in free will and free choice. It would be a combination of both. For, we assure you, the ego-personality would not be set aside by soul-essence. It would be the equivalent of you setting aside your complete left side in order to allow your right side to go left. It's an impossibility.

There could be some other energy creating an opportunity for you to observe and an opportunity for choice, yes. However, it is always your free will and free choice that chooses to explore the opportunities. View it from this perspective: We've suggested to each of you to observe your existence, to observe all aspects of your existence. Now, from that perspective, when you observe existence, you begin to observe opportunities of your existence. The opportunities create opportunities for free will and free choice. Those opportunities were created by yourselves, attracted by yourselves through the use of the mind. The mind is a tool. You use the mind to create opportunities to attract other opportunities to yourselves. Therefore, the mind, which is the seed or the basis of the seed of thought, is the creator of opportunities in your existence. The ability to use free will and free choice to choose to think is your first opportunity in applying free will and free choice in your existence. Most individuals, yourselves included, often leave the mind to its own devices. Therefore, the mind creates based on its own perceptions, its own free will and free choice. You've extended free will and free choice to the mind, and not given it direction. Therefore, the mind moves here, the mind moves there, often creating circumstances and situations that cause havoc in your existence. There is less benefit. And then you wonder why these particular circumstances and situations occur in your existence. It's because you have chosen to not choose, which is also a choice.

On ways to perceive the totality of existence beyond the five senses

The other methodology for realizing the totality of existence, apart from tapping into soul-essence, is to open yourself to the awareness of other existences.

View it from this perspective. As a result of regressions in which you've experienced other existences, you've become aware of the experience of another existence. You've expanded yourselves to open yourselves to that awareness. You use the word *regression* to define an experience of moving outward from this particular experience to that particular experience. Regression is not a true definition; another word would be more appropriate. However, to use that particular word, do not use it as a limiting factor of viewing regression as simply viewing the past. It is simply viewing existence from a different perspective. Therefore, allow yourselves to experience the opportunity to view other existences as an expansion of your awareness.

Now, if you choose, you can also reconnect with soul-essence, and soul-essence will be more than glad to provide you with an awareness of knowledge and existence. Most individuals are not prepared to do this. But we assure each and every one of you that you can do this in this lifetime. You're not limited to this particular lifetime. Though this lifetime has a limited perspective, for each of you will cast off feet of clay, we assure you, there is not a limitation to your experience.

How you experience this lifetime is up to you. You can choose to experience it as a ditch digger, and that would be the extent of your experience. Or you can choose to experience it as a soul-essence, and that would be the extent of your experience.

Now, in order to get a sense of what it's like to feel beyond the five senses, view it from this perspective: Simply describe your sixth sense, a sense of awareness of existence. When you walk through your residence or on the street, you are aware of energy patterns, energy movements, are you not? Not consciously. Not always. But sometimes you open yourselves sufficiently to become aware of patterns and interconnections. And at that point, you expand yourselves. There's another sense.

There are many more senses. However, if we were to describe to you that particular perspective of senses—the seventh, the eighth, the ninth, the tenth, in fact, almost the eighty-seventh sense—what we would be describing to you is oneness. And we assure you, at this point, you cannot yet grasp the concept or the perspective of the totality of oneness. You intellectualize it, you see it from the perspective of "there is one." But what does it mean to be at one with all existence? How does that feel? What does it represent? What is the beingness of being interconnected? To experience oneness is to be totally connected, not more connected.

View it from this perspective: Allow us to extend our energy outward for a moment. Now, observe how each and every one of you describes your experience of interconnectedness differently. Each one of you perceived it based on your perception of judgment of yourself. You experienced the experience through the filter of self-judgment. Interesting, isn't it? Yet, each one of you experienced the same energy.

To provide you with a perspective that was not based on self-judgment, you would have to be willing to set aside self-judgment. Self-judgment limited you to the experience of the experience, limited you to the description of your experience. You felt a certain energy flow, a certain warmth–in some cases, a chakra opening. Each of you experienced the same energy from a different perspective. The reason you experienced it differently is that each of you has a different perspective of your own existence, a different self-judgment. Now, set aside judgment, and it simply is. Had you then experienced the energy without self-judgment, you would have experienced existence.

We assure you, the more self-judgment you set aside, the greater the expansion of your experience of existence. And the greater the expansion of the experience of your existence, the greater the perception of manifested spirit in your existence.

Now, allow us to do this. We will extend ourselves outward once again for a period of approximately thirty seconds. Observe yourselves. Notice how each and every one of you has extended your experience of existence. Second experience, same energy, and you still judged. For each and every one of you has still judged the experience based on your own self-judgment. Yet you've set aside an infinitesimal portion of self-judgment, sufficient to allow yourselves to expand the limit of your experience. Now, the more you do that, the broader the experience. Do you see what we're saying here? Interesting, isn't it?

Let's do this one last time. As we extend our energy, we will provide you with another stimulus, one that will affect your five physical senses. What we would like you to do is to observe the stimulus and allow yourselves to interconnect with each other so sufficiently that you will experience the same experience.

Each and every one of you, though you were prepared to observe the experience as we suggested, chose to observe it with judgment. Each one of you observed it from one perspective or another, attempting to expand your perception without judgment, yet you still used judgment in the observation without judgment. Having said that, if you observe carefully, each and every one of you had the same experience. Each one of you simply described it differently, yet you allowed yourself to experience the experience equivalently.

View it from this perspective: You've asked us questions about existence being an extension of the self. You've just experienced existence as an extension of yourselves through your filters, your perceptions designed and accepted by your free will and your free choice to apply that which you chose to perceive in the moment on the basis of the experience of existence.

There is an awareness within yourselves of the experience of the existence that goes beyond the five physical senses. Each of you has an awareness of an experience–that it came through the five senses, true. But the awareness exists beyond the five senses. Therefore, the awareness of yourselves beyond the five senses is a doorway to preparing you to expand your own perceptions of yourselves to that which you truly are, which is soul-essence.

CHAPTER TWO

I Am Sufficient

The Second Defining Statement

The statement, "I Am Sufficient," is a statement that will alter and shift the reality of your existence, if you but begin to observe it. Those of you who are reading this book will begin to recognize that, through observation, you will then observe your sufficiency.

Now, what does it mean to be sufficient? View it from this perspective: The fisherman who catches only one fish is sufficient. The fisherman who catches one million fish is sufficient. The hooker down the street is sufficient. The priest is sufficient. The minister is sufficient. The politician is sufficient. The poor man walking the streets, sleeping on the street is sufficient. The individual, the housewife, the son, the daughter, the father–all are sufficient. Viewed from this perspective, there is not an insufficiency that exists in anyone. Yet most individuals spend a great deal of their existence attempting to understand their insufficiencies rather than observing their sufficiencies.

They view themselves not from the perspective of sufficient, but rather from the perspective of insufficient. They look at themselves and say, "I'm not as good as. I can't do this, I can't do that. I can't think, I can't read, I can't accomplish, I can't speak. I can't, I can't, I can't." The phrase "I can't" becomes their mantra, in effect. They spend the majority of their existence telling themselves what they cannot do, accomplish or become, and at no time do they examine and observe that which they can do–that which they are. As a result, they never discover their sufficiency. They never discover that in a certain set of circumstances, in a certain situation–regardless of the circumstance or situation–they have the talents, the abilities, the awareness and the wherewithal to interact with that circumstance or situation in a fashion that is beneficial for themselves.

As a result, they perceive themselves as "insufficient." But if you just begin to observe yourselves from the perspective of the statement, "I am sufficient," then, dear friends, you open yourselves to the unlimitedness that you are. Eventually, this will lead you to the third statement of our series.

The "I Am" in the statement doesn't say "you are." It

doesn't say "he is," or "she is," or "it is." It says "I." What is *I* to the self, but the totality of the self. What is *I* to the ego, to the personality, but the amalgamation, in effect, of all that comprises the ego and the personality–each part becoming *I* and therefore forming the whole of *I*, each individual part sufficient in and of itself. From one perspective, the "I" can viewed as a broad-stroke *I* or viewed as a very defined *I*. It can be viewed as a part of ego-personality. It can be viewed as the whole of ego-personality. And if you choose, it can be viewed beyond ego-personality to include the soul-essence, the totality of that which you are–that which we often describe as the "you that is you." We use the words *the you that is you* as a way for individuals to recognize that there is a greater aspect–that of the self–that encompasses all aspects of the self. And therefore, from that perspective, the *I* resonates to it.

Am–let's look at that word. It doesn't say "might be," "could be," "will be," "should be," "ought to be," "possibly," "maybe," "in another lifetime," "in the future" or "in the past." It doesn't talk about what was or what will be. *Am* speaks directly to the instant of the moment, the very instant of this moment. Therefore, dear friends, "I Am" resonates and speaks to the moment of existence in which you find yourselves.

Now, when you reflect on the moment that was, does that mean that "I Am" no longer applies? Quite the contrary. "I Am" applies to the moment that was and the moment that is. For in the moment that is, you are reflecting on the moment that was, and therefore, "I Am" still applies.

Thus, when you find yourselves observing—or, in the reflection of your observance, when you find yourselves looking back over the choices you have made, the existence you have lived, the circumstances you have found yourselves in, the directions you have chosen as a result of these particular events—when you find yourselves in this aspect of reflection, recognize that "I Am" applies.

And when you think to yourselves of what will be, of the direction you are choosing, the choices you are making now that will move you in the certain direction you would like to go, what you would like to do and how you would like to be—when you find yourselves reflecting on those moments—recognize that in the moment of reflection, "I Am" applies.

Notice that we've only spoken of two small words, three letters in total. And yet those three letters, joined together to form two words, are so powerful as to bring you back to the moment of existence.

Now, add to those powerful words, those powerful letters, another set of letters that comprise a word, the word *sufficient.* Sufficient means there is nothing lacking, that all that is needed exists. It is complete. It is whole. It is absolute. It is without lack, without denigration, without reduction. It is total. And from that perspective, therefore, it could be said, it is love.

Therefore, when you view yourselves as sufficient, when you observe yourselves as sufficient—regardless of the moment you observe, the circumstances you observe, the response you observe—you will recognize that you, dear friends, are sufficient. You will recognize that you have the total of all necessity in the moment, and that you, dear friends, are the total of that necessity. You don't lack. You're not missing. There's nothing to denigrate. There's nothing that does not apply.

Therefore, when you find yourselves in a circumstance whereby anger begins to degenerate it, when you find yourselves angry, instead of seeing yourselves as "less than" because anger exists within you, instead of reflecting on your anger as being something that is lacking within yourselves, instead of using the anger as a way of denigrating not only others but also yourselves—may we suggest, dear friends, that you observe your sufficiency in the moment. Recognize how sufficient you are. Recognize that you have anger, true; that it forms part of that which you are in that moment, true. But that does not reduce you. It does not eliminate from you. It does not denigrate you. For in truth, in that very instant when you are hotly angry, ready to rip off another person's head with your words or actions, you are sufficient.

This statement that is given to you is a statement that has no limits. It isn't designed for you, dear friends, as ego-personalities, to say to yourselves, "In this situation, I am sufficient. In that situation, I'm not quite as sufficient. And that individual over there, well, he's not sufficient at all." We assure you, this is not what it is designed to do. For in truth, once you've observed how sufficient you are, regardless of the circumstances of your existence, you will also recognize the sufficiency of another. All are sufficient.

This statement will alter your existence. It will alter the way you move through your existence. And those of you here, we assure you that the moment the statement was made to yourselves and you began to observe it, you were on a journey that was unable to be altered. In other words, you were on an unalterable journey of self-discovery.

And why not? Why not discover how sufficient you are in the moment? Why not discover how sufficient you are in relationships? Why not discover how sufficient you are at playing tennis, badminton, hockey, baseball, softball, pinochle, chess? Why not discover how sufficient you are at work, doing whatever you do in a work environment? Why not discover how sufficient you are simply sitting on top of a mountain and gazing at your navel? For then too, you are sufficient.

Being sufficient—the statement, "I Am Sufficient"—is not about going out and doing, for you are sufficient in the doing. It is not about going out and being, for you are sufficient in the being. It does not take sides. It does not define and limit the self. It expands and broadens the perspective of the self. Begin to allow yourselves the opportunity to discover your sufficiency, dear friends, and you will recognize that it is through choice that you limit your perspective of your sufficiency–your choice, not another's choice. It is through your choice that you limit your perspective of your sufficiency.

And we repeat this again–it is through your choice that you limit your perspective of your sufficiency. Hear the words carefully, dear friends. When you see yourselves as "not quite as good as," then you limit your perspective of your sufficiency. When you see another as being "not quite as good as," then you limit your perspective of your sufficiency.

Notice, we said *your* sufficiency. We didn't say another's, here. When you judge another, you limit your perspective of your sufficiency. When you judge anything, animate or inanimate, with yourself, by yourself, you limit your perspective of your sufficiency.

View it from this perspective: You're walking through the forest. Trees surround you–evergreens, maples, elms, birch trees, they all surround you. Leaves are on the forest floor. Squirrels, mice, rabbits, deer, all live in the forest. As you walk through the forest, you find yourselves unable to appreciate your surroundings. You find yourselves uneasy. Fear begins to set in. What if there are bears? What if there are wolves? How would you deal with them?

At that point, you've begun to observe your insufficiency, not your sufficiency, for you begin to doubt yourselves. You begin to judge yourselves by judging your surroundings. For if it be truly observed, you would recognize, dear friends, that regardless of circumstances–whether there were bears surrounding you, or wolves, or anything else–you are sufficient. You would recognize that that which you are is sufficient to deal with the circumstances presented to you. When you view yourselves from that perspective, you begin to set fear aside. For there can be no perspective of sufficiency where fear exists. Fear reduces the perspective of sufficiency and moves it to a perspective of insufficiency. We assure you, for when you see yourselves as "I am sufficient," you will begin to set aside the fears that limit, control and reduce your existence.

Now, that's not to say you would immediately run up and jump off a cliff in the hopes that you will fly, saying to yourself, "I am sufficient, I am sufficient, I am sufficient"–splat–"Oh dear, I guess I wasn't." This isn't about that. It isn't about going out and proving to yourself that you are something you are not. It is about accepting that which you are. If as an individual, you decided to jump off a cliff in order to fly, you would soon find out that you're not a bird. And we assure you, the result would not be pretty. Birds fly. Unfortunately, humans have yet to discover that they too can fly.

And will they? No–their arms are too big. Not enough feathers.

Therefore, don't go out and attempt to prove to yourself that you're something you are not. However, do recognize that that which you are is sufficient. In other words, it isn't that you need to jump off the cliff and pretend to be a bird in order to fly, but that you are a human being with a mind capable of devising and creating a certain material object that would assist you in flying. That is to your credit. You are sufficient.

When countries go to war, when people–through the use of, the excuse of, war–go out and kill each other, they are then proving to themselves that they are insufficient. The conqueror and the vanquished are as insufficient, one as the other. And they prove it to themselves. How? Because both had to view themselves as either "greater than" or "less than" in order to justify their actions to themselves. They had to justify their choices. They did not choose simply to be and therefore, simply make the choices they made. They did not see themselves as being sufficient in the moment. Yet they were. Whether you kill or whether you love, you are still sufficient. And that's the key here, dear friends. It's that, in your existence, you spend a great deal of your energy proving to yourselves your insufficiency and–once again, we will repeat–you never observe your sufficiency.

Your sufficiency is the basis of your existence. It is that which moves you from here to there. It is that which connects you to all of existence. It is that which is that which you are. It is the energy of beingness. It is universal energy, which is that which you are. It is, from one perspective, all of that which you are–all of existence.

Yet through your choices, you choose to confirm to

yourselves your insufficiency in order to prove to yourselves that you are not sufficient. And why do you do this? You do this, dear friends, because you fear being sufficient. You fear it with every breath you take, every bone in your body, every cell of your physical self, every aspect of your physical, mental and emotional self. You fear your sufficiency.

For if you were to accept your sufficiency, then, dear friends, you would exist in a state of love—of pure, absolute, total self-love. And that, dear friends, you find unacceptable. For if you were in a state of pure, total, absolute self-love, there would not be conflict within yourselves. And that game is one you really enjoy playing.

So better not to observe your sufficiency and to reinforce your insufficiency so that you can keep on playing the game of self-destruction, of reduction. Because after all, it's the game you know, the rules you've always played by. It's the fun you have in your existence. Your whole existence is designed to pleasure yourselves.

How do you pleasure yourselves? By hurting yourselves, by hating yourselves—in effect, by reducing yourselves. These words sound rather strong, don't they? But we assure you, dear friends, observe your existence, and you will recognize how much of yourselves you see as insufficient and how much energy you spend proving it to yourselves. Vast amounts of energy.

In fact, if we took one person and accumulated all of the energy that person has spent over a lifetime to prove his insufficiency to himself, from the time he was born to the time he cast off feet of clay—on an average life span of 72.3 years, that individual could build ten cities with that energy. Ten cities of approximately 328,000 people (to give you limits, to make it in a definable, acceptable way for you). Think about it. Ten cities of 328,000 people with skyscrapers, with roads, with infrastructure, with houses, with electricity. The energy to build ten cities is what you expend in a lifetime to prove to yourselves how insufficient you are.

May we suggest here, dear friends: Change it around. Spend one-one thousandth of that energy to observe how sufficient you are and use the rest to build ten more cities. A lot more fun.

"I Am Sufficient." That doesn't say, "I am less than." It doesn't say, "I am more than." "I'm better than he is, I'm better than she is." "I'm not as good as he is, I'm not as good as she is." It doesn't say, "I can't be an Indian chief," "I can't be a politician, a sailor, a doctor, a dentist." It says, "I Am Sufficient." Nothing more, nothing less.

Notice the energy of those words. It doesn't take a great deal of energy to say, "I Am Sufficient." But recognize how much energy it takes to say, "I am less than"; "I am more than"; "I'm better than you"; "I'm less than you." Notice the amount of energy you expend in those philosophies, those phrases, those belief structures.

If you were to begin to shift your consciousness such that you viewed yourselves as sufficient, and you shared this perspective with your children, and the children of your children, and the children of the children of your children, then we assure you, dear friends, that within less than eight generations, society itself would move to that perspective of sufficiency.

One individual alone will move the generation resulting from that individual. Not all of society will change. But share your perspective of sufficiency such that others also observe their sufficiency. Share it. Let others see how you perceive yourselves and how you struggle with your concepts, your ideas, your perceptions of your own sufficiency.

For you will struggle, dear friends. Why do we say this? Why would we, The Wonders, give you a statement and say to you, "This will be hard. This will be tough?" Because, dear friends, if we didn't say to you that this would be hard, this would be tough, you'd never spend time observing your sufficiency. You like hard, tough things to do. It is part of what you are.

If we were to say to you that this would be so easy; all you have to do is observe it once and it will permeate your existence–we assure you, you would never do it. You'd sit there and say to yourselves, "Oh dear, why bother? I can do it tomorrow. If all I have to do is do it once, why do it now? I can do it tomorrow, the day after. There's plenty of time." And so you never would.

So instead, we assure you, dear friends, this is the toughest thing you will ever do. You will struggle. You will fight. In effect, you will struggle to hold onto your beliefs of insufficiency. You want them. You love them. You honor them. They've been your best friends all your lives. They are what has kept you alive. Not this simple little concept of "I Am Sufficient," far from it. It is all this convoluted concept of how little you are, how less you are, how greater you are, how lacking you are. That is what has kept you alive. That is what has given you your breath. And so it goes. That concept, that philosophy, those ideas, you will hang on to dearly.

But we assure you, the power of the words, "I Am Sufficient," will not be denied. You cannot ever deny your sufficiency. Oh, you can deny it for a period of time, as you've done for many lifetimes, we assure you. And you can deny it for today and tomorrow and the day after that. But eventually, you will begin to observe your sufficiency.

The key is that when you begin to observe it, don't observe it for a moment and say, "Well, that was good. Oh dear, don't need to do this again. Know it all." We assure you, far from it. This statement itself is designed to go through all the layers of the self, all the aspects of the self, such that no one layer, no one aspect, no one part of the totality of that which you are will remain untouched by this statement. Picture it as a never-stopping, totally energized little burrower, one that will burrow its way through every aspect of yourselves. It will leave no part untouched, unturned, ignored, denied, denigrated, reduced. None.

Now, what do you say to that? What do you say to the possibility, the probability, the awareness that that which you are, you will finally come to recognize in its totality; that you have begun a journey that is irrevocable, that cannot be altered. It can be delayed, true. But it cannot be altered.

View it from this perspective: Both dear Maggie and this one have been on a journey of discovering their sufficiency for the last 823 lifetimes. And they still have yet to discover the totality of their sufficiency. But as they are both aware in this lifetime, they will not stop, slow down, deny, set aside that part of themselves anymore. We assure you, they are intent to uncover every part they've ever left uncovered previously. That is to their credit.

You can, too. In fact, there are some here this evening who are also doing the same. Their journeys are different. The results are the same. Dear Maggie and this one are not unique. But they are sufficient. And that is key. As so are you—all of you. No one less and no one more than the other.

Now, we've gone to a great deal of energy and expended a little bit of effort here to describe sufficiency to you. We've described it, we've given you ideas and perspectives in regards to it. And we are certain, dear friends, that when you reflect, each and every one of you, you will come up with a million more opportunities to define sufficiency, for there are no limits to it.

Therefore, may we suggest that, if you choose, you spend the time to observe your sufficiency in the next few moments as we move you through a certain meditation, a perspective that will assist you in discovering this sufficiency.

Meditation to assist you in observing your sufficiency

Now, we would suggest that you please find a relaxing position. And when you are ready, set aside all paper, pens and items. Calm the mind and take three very deep breaths. And we say three, because we like the number three.

As you move your consciousness to a space of relaxation, allow the mind to quiet sufficiently to begin to observe your surroundings. Open your eyes, without losing your quietness, and look around you. Observe your surroundings. Observe yourselves in your sitting or lying-down positions, in your relaxed state. Observe your bodies. Observe that which surrounds you. And quietly, calmly, once you've observed, close the eyes, such that the observations remain in the mind.

Allow the mind then to expand, to expand its perspective beyond that which you have seen through the eyes. Move the consciousness to encompass the room you are in, the house or dwelling you are in, the environment outside, the environment surrounding you. Expand your consciousness to recognize the trees, the wind blowing through the leaves, the birds singing in the trees, the grass bending as the breeze gently flaps over it. The ants busily working.

Expand your consciousness to see beyond the physical realm. Move the consciousness outward, such that the consciousness begins to observe the interrelationship of energy as it moves through the physical realm. As it moves through the trees, see the energy moving, surrounding you, playing like a child plays. See the energy as it moves through your consciousness–how energy threads move from your consciousness outward and attach themselves to those physical surroundings.

Let yourselves observe without judgment. Simply observe how the energy surrounds you, envelops you, holds you, forms a part of that which you are. And in that, expand your consciousness such that you discover that the energy surrounding you, enveloping you, is a part of that which you are. That it comes from within that which you are–from within the center of your heart chakra, moving out from your seventh, crown chakra and enveloping and surrounding you. It moves through each chakra, never remaining in one but encompassing all.

And observe how the energy that surrounds you is an energy of compassion, an energy of love and an energy of sufficiency. That that which you observe is sufficient. Observe that there is nothing lacking, that there is nothing missing. Observe the totality of the energy as it moves. Observe how it interrelates to all that exists, and how you interrelate to that energy itself.

Observe how your energy moves to the energy of those surrounding you–family, friends, acquaintances, whether they be physically near you or at a distance.

Let yourselves flow without fear, without judgment. Just note how energy itself encompasses you. And if you choose, observe the energy that surrounds the energy that you are. Expand your consciousness to observe this energy and to observe that that energy is also sufficient, that there is nothing lacking. That it is whole and complete and that it encompasses all that you are.

Observe how your wholeness, your completeness, intertwines itself with the energy that is beyond you, and how your wholeness and completeness form a part of the wholeness and completeness that is beyond the self.

And love it. Extend yourselves outward to it. Perceive, through your observation, the sufficiency of everything that exists. And observe yourselves as being an integral part of that which is sufficient.

Allow your consciousness to play with the energy, to move with it. As it flows here, flow with it. As it flows there, go with it. Allow yourselves simply to be as the wind itself–without direction, yet sufficient. With all the awareness and knowledge necessary to be that which you are.

And once you've enjoyed this observation and once you've observed that sufficiency, bring back with you to your consciousness the awareness of your integral connection to all of existence, that you too will recognize your sufficiency as you've recognized its sufficiency.

And now, if you choose, you can take a period of time to play with this energy and observe it. If you choose, give yourselves that time.

May we suggest that you are sufficient now to return to the moment. Bring your consciousness back, and in bringing it back, recognize that that which you have observed–that which has formed part of that which you are–has expanded that which you are in such a way that that which you are is sufficient, is never lacking, always is. And that, if you choose, you can always return to this moment such that you can explore your degrees of sufficiency to your benefit.

And now, dear friends, please take three deep breaths and return yourselves to the moment.

✷ ✷ ✷

Now that you've begun to observe through meditation that which we spoke of–the statement, "I Am Sufficient"–recognize that you can do this anytime, anywhere. We would suggest, however, that you don't close your eyes when you're driving. Keep your eyes open. But you can extend your consciousness. That you can do.

In the meditation, notice that that which you've observed with your eyes expanded your consciousness.

It didn't limit. Why? Because you, dear friends, are sufficient. Nothing reduces you. Nothing takes away from you. No one, no thing, reduces, eliminates or denigrates that which you are.

Therefore, once you perceive yourselves as sufficient, we assure you, you cannot be harmed. Harm comes to you when you see yourselves as insufficient. See yourselves as sufficient, and you will never be harmed–not physically, not mentally, not emotionally and not spiritually. And once you've observed your sufficiency sufficiently, then you will discover the interconnection of yourselves to all of your past, present and future lives, such that, through observation, you will gain an appreciation of yourselves and the totality of all your existences, how each are intertwined with the moment you are in.

We give you this gift of a meditation that you may, if you choose, use it to your greater benefit. However, we assure you, dear friends, to each and every one of you, you are sufficient. There is nothing lacking within you.

The meditation was designed to expand that which you are if you chose to. You do not expand on the basis of lack. You do not take something and make it greater on the basis that it is missing something. You take something that is whole and complete, give it love and watch it grow. And that, dear friends, is what you are. That is your sufficiency. That which you are is sufficient. And given love, given the perspective of your sufficiency, you then can gain a new awareness of your sufficiency.

And we assure you—each and every one of you—you will.

Additional Comments

On being sufficient

When you perceive yourselves as sufficient, it isn't that you perceive yourselves as having degrees of sufficiency. We often suggest that you view your existence as a degree of benefit rather than a perspective of judgment, of right or wrong, good or bad. The reason we give that perspective is to expand your consciousness.

However, recognize that there is no degree to the concept of "I Am Sufficient." There simply is "I Am Sufficient." Regardless of circumstance, regardless of situation, that which you are is sufficient. Therefore, it isn't that you change and you grow, that you alter the sufficiency. It is that you are sufficient—plain, pure and simple. It cannot be expressed any other way. You are sufficient. We are sufficient. God/Goddess/The All That Is is sufficient.

The need within yourselves to measure the degrees of sufficiency is based on your perception of your insufficiency. Once you perceive yourselves as sufficient, you will recognize that there is no necessity to view the concept of sufficiency in degrees. There's no validity, there is no expansion of that particular concept. There simply is the statement. And we assure you, you will move there once you choose to allow yourselves to move to that statement.

Your purpose here is to discover your sufficiency, since, though you were sufficient, you did not perceive yourselves as such. It isn't that that which you are has altered or shifted or changed. It is that your perception of that which you are has altered, shifted and changed. Your perception of your insufficiency, or your sufficiency, has shifted and altered. You don't perceive yourselves as sufficient. But that which you are is sufficient. In effect, you are therefore relearning your sufficiency. By relearning, you expand to the perception of that which you are.

View it from this perspective: Take a point. That point is sufficient. It is all-inclusive. There is nothing missing. It is a point. However, a point on the point does not see itself as the point. It sees only a portion of itself. Therefore, it wants to grow and expand to see itself completely. So it sends out its consciousness in a never-ending circle of expansion to discover itself. Eventually, it sends out its consciousness sufficiently to discover that it isn't a point, but it is a point on a point, and therefore it can move to the concept of becoming the point. At that point, it becomes the point, and then there is no point to this particular conversation.

It isn't that you become sufficient, dear friends; it is that you become aware of your sufficiency. We did say that this is a defining statement of your existence. Your existence is defined as "I Am Sufficient." That is your existence. An existence isn't necessarily limited to ego-personality existence. It is your existence, that which you are, which comprises all aspects of your ego-personality: the conscious, the subconscious, the superconscious, the soul-essence, the high self–however you wish to describe it-as well as God/Goddess/The All That Is. Therefore, you are on a journey of rediscovery, or self-discovery, of discovering that the point that "you are" is the only point to all of this point conversation. That is the point. Interesting, isn't it? Now, we use semantics here, we use a few words to bring levity to the circumstance. But recognize that you are reawaking, relearning, reobserving that that which you are is that which you are.

There is a degree of awareness within you, but it has been clouded over by perceptions, by misunderstandings, misperceptions, fear and illusion. Therefore, you find yourselves caught up with a certain illusion that you think represents your existence, which in truth only represents the point on the point. You choose to do this, not just as soul-essence, but also as ego-personality, for you do have free choice and free will as ego-personality. Yes, soul-essence chooses. Yes, God/Goddess/The All That Is chooses. And every dimension of existence chooses.

Take it from this perspective. If you take a pencil and make a point on a piece of paper, that point is complete and whole. It doesn't need anything more. However, as ego-personalities, you think you need more. Therefore, you go out searching for more and draw a big circle around that small point, and you look outward, seeking to find yourselves. And when you draw the big circle, you try to define yourselves as that big circle. Eventually, you'll get to the point of recognizing that that big circle is the point the pencil made.

But until you perceive that, you will always see yourselves as moving through degrees of sufficiency. Once you perceive yourselves as sufficient, you will recognize your interconnection to all existence. However, it isn't that they are equivalent; it is that they are the same. As we did say with regards to the point of the pencil and the circle around it, you're looking out to discover the circle only to find out that it was the point that began it.

You are connected to all existence because you are all existence. That which you see as separate from yourselves is only separate because of your perception of separateness. It isn't separate; it is that which you are. For example, we ourselves are a twenty-ninth-dimension reality consciousness. That which separates us from God/Goddess/The All That Is on the thirty-second dimension is a perception of separateness. That perception is minimal, true, but it still exists. Otherwise, we would be God/Goddess/The All That Is. And we, in our own way, are moving through that particular perception to set that perception aside. But there is still a perception of separateness. You see yourselves as separate from ourselves. Yet you are not. You are that which we are. We assure you, from one perspective, there is no separateness between ourselves and yourselves. It is simply that you perceive yourselves as separate. And as long as you maintain the perception of separateness, you will never see yourselves as that which we are.

This statement, "I Am Sufficient," will assist you in lifting the veils of separateness, in setting aside the illusion that that which you are isn't sufficient. There is another statement that we will examine, and that statement is, "That Which You Are Is That Which I Am, and That Which I Am Is That Which You Are." The reason we choose to discuss it is because you are ready, both as a group and as individuals, to explore beyond the limits of your individuality, your separateness, to the limits of a group. As you do so, you will discover that there is nothing separating you from another—or from ourselves, in fact—other than perception. Move beyond the perception, and you move beyond the illusion of separateness.

The statement, "I Am Sufficient," allows you to recognize that you are "that which is," and "that which is" is that which you are. The only reason you doubt your ability to achieve a perception of sufficiency, dear friends, is that you enjoy reveling, rolling in, wrestling in the mud of insufficiency. We would suggest that you can continue and have fun. Or you can step out of the ring and have more fun.

On third-dimensional reality and the illusion of separateness

Recognize that you begin with the illusion of separateness. You do not manifest yourself in third-dimensional reality as a direct extension of God/ Goddess/The All That Is from the thirty-second dimension. You manifest yourself as an extension of an extension of an extension of an extension. As a result, you begin from the perspective of separateness. True, it is a broader perspective than that which you perceive in third-dimensional reality. But it is still a perspective of separateness.

One of the reasons you reincarnate in third-dimensional reality is that you wish to observe the perspective of separateness to such a degree as to then recognize your perspective of separateness as soul-essence. Your soul-essence perceives itself as separate from God/ Goddess/The All That Is. It chooses to incarnate you in order to observe, through the observation of incarnation, the aspects that define separateness in order for it to uncover within itself the perspective that it believes are the illusions under which it exists.

We ourselves in the twenty-ninth dimension of reality are not God/Goddess/The All That Is, we assure you. We do have an illusion of separateness that is maintained within ourselves that we are moving through to eliminate or to uncover, to rediscover. From a soul-essence perspective, however, that which we are is God/Goddess/The All That Is. That which we are has ego, true–an equivalent of ego-personality. And God/Goddess/The All That Is has ego. It is only that the ego has achieved a certain degree of balance within the totality of that which we are, such that it is not that which we are. As a result, we see ourselves as a collective. We use the term collective consciousness as a way of describing ourselves in a manner that is sufficient for your consciousness to accept. For there are no accurate words that would describe the totality of that which we are. Collective consciousness comes the closest. As a result, that which we are is still separate from God/Goddess/The All That Is. From that perspective, we could be said to have a soul-essence. That soul-essence is God/Goddess/The All That Is. Therefore, we still move ourselves to rediscover the totality of that which we are without separation from God/Goddess/The All That Is.

On the statement, "I Am Sufficient," and its effect on soul-essence growth

Each soul-essence, each dimensional reality of existence, is based on a limited perception of the term "I Am Sufficient." Remember what we said: That which you are is sufficient. It is only that you see yourselves as insufficient that you maintain a certain degree of separateness from God/Goddess/The All That Is. Soul-essences are no different than you are, dear friends.

Their perspective is broader; they have a greater understanding of the universe, a greater awareness of all existence. However, it's greater only in the sense that they recognize and have uncovered—lifted—the veils of illusion slightly. But they still see themselves as insufficient. If they didn't, they would then see themselves as God/Goddess/The All That Is. We ourselves are also insufficient, to a degree. For if we did not perceive ourselves with a certain degree of insufficiency, we would be God/Goddess/The All That Is.

Interesting, isn't it? Therefore, we are no different than you. The statement, "I Am Sufficient," describes God/Goddess/The All That Is, and we are all striving to see that sufficiency in every aspect of existence. The more you allow yourselves to explore the concept defined by the statement, "I Am Sufficient," the more you will explore your limitlessness—which brings us to the third statement: "I Am Limitless; My Choices Reflect My Limitlessness."

On the impact of viewing oneself as sufficient in everyday life

When one sees himself as sufficient, he sees himself as being interconnected to all of existence. The choice to belong to existence is a choice made. If taxes are part of that existence, then taxes are part of the choice. However, that does not mean you accept the level of taxation. If you, in your perception, perceive that taxation is too strong, too great or too little, then you, dear friends, can choose to alter that perception. You then become sufficient to make that choice, make that shift, make that change. In other words, your desires are sufficient; they are not limited by your needs. When you perceive yourselves as wanting to satisfy your needs and that your desires are not satisfied, you limit your desire by need. Most individuals do. They limit their desire on the basis of need. When you see yourselves as sufficient, you see yourselves as able to receive your desires.

Interesting, isn't it? Therefore, if you desire no taxes, you can receive no taxes. When you get to the point of seeing yourselves as sufficient, you're simply in a position to keep choosing. And why would you choose to pay taxes? Some would, for they see a benefit to society. But when you perceive your sufficiency, you will also recognize that the benefit is limited and is based on perceptions of power. Taxation does not benefit society, we assure you. As much as individuals would like you to believe this, it benefits the individuals that do the taxation.

Society does not grow as a result of taxation; society grows as a result of a willingness by individuals to allow growth–to make it grow. Voluntary assistance by individuals is what makes society grow, not taxation. Taxation has never allowed a society grow. It has reduced society. Witness Canadian or American society. Witness any society on this planet where taxation exists, and we assure you, those societies do not grow. Take a look at the example in the Canadian provinces. In those provinces where taxation is limited or is being reduced, the economy is growing. In those provinces where taxation is increasing, the economy is slowing. Society does not grow by taxation. It does not stop crime. It does not stop reduction, disconnection, denigration of another. Taxation does none of that.

View it from this perspective: Far be it for ourselves to advocate anarchy here; however, why are you taxed? You're taxed because you choose to allow it. We would suggest, change it. Stop it. We assure you that this concept is already part of the mass consciousness that exists in North American society. There is a movement underfoot here to reduce taxes. Observe your politicians, observe how they're squirming in the federal cabinet right now. They have a certain amount of money, but instead of reducing the debt, they're looking to spend it. Why? Because that way they can maintain the level of taxation. Why do they need to maintain the level of taxation? Because that is the only game they know how to play.

You can stop it in the sense of lobbying, voting for people and having it changed. That's one way to stop it. Another way is, don't file your tax return. You don't get taxed on what they don't know about. Part of you knows that if you simply do not pay, you will not be taxed. If you do not file, you will not be taxed. However, you fear not filing; you fear not paying. As a result, you're taxed. Set aside the fear.

Now, we're not advocating anarchy, as we did say. This isn't about that. If, however, you wish to be part of society and you see yourselves as sufficient, then you also see yourselves as sufficient to alter and shift society. Therefore, we would suggest that although you perceive it as a long process, it isn't long, we assure you. It just requires the right amount of energy applied at the right time to shift circumstances.

On the impact of viewing oneself as sufficient in terms of power struggles within relationships

Stop playing the game. The individual who wants to manipulate you because he needs to see himself—or herself, for that matter—as greater than, and therefore manipulates and attempts to control your existence, he only does so because you play the game. It's like ping-pong. He hits the ball, you send it back. He hits the ball, you send it back. We're saying, put down your paddle and leave the table. Don't play the game. If you have a boss making your life miserable, it's because you let him make your life miserable. You are attached to his actions. In other words, you're hitting the ball back every time. We're saying, stop playing the game. Ignore, and step aside. Don't let it be part of your existence. And if as a result of this, he gets so angry, so frustrated, that he fires you, then you respond.

When you find yourself in a game, dear friends—and it's usually a good game of ping-pong, we assure you—you have a choice. You can keep on hitting the ball as best you can. You can hone your talents and abilities and play the ball even better. You can get a bigger paddle, a better paddle, and therefore play a better game. All of this is fun, and all of this will lead you to a degree of benefit. However, the one solution you've never thought of is to say to yourself, "I quit." In other words, walk away. Stop playing the game. Then the individual is left playing with himself. Which is a concept that is quite interesting, in and of itself.

Think of it this way. One man, one paddle, two balls—could be interesting. He needs two because, unfortunately, the first one doesn't get sent back. Do you see? Stop playing the game. We assure you, this is an option. Most individuals don't think of it, and when they do, they discard it. Why? Because they enjoy playing the game. They like to prove to themselves that their talents are such that they can play the game. And so they continue until eventually, out of frustration, out of whatever, they find themselves so totally destroyed that they finally say, "I give up." When they give up, they're saying, "I quit," in effect. We're suggesting, why wait until you're totally beaten into the ground before you say, "I quit?"

The same applies to the controlling methods of mass media. When someone says to you, "For the next fifty-six minutes, we can sell you the most wonderful thing you can ever think of. We will be able to tell you how much money you can make. We can send you all this information. We can send it to you postage paid. And for you, dear friends, only 3,700 payments at $12.95 a month." Think of it. Then, dear friends, all you need to say is, "Thank you. I quit. Good-bye." In fact, if you choose, don't even say good-bye.

Interesting, isn't it? What would you do if, when you wanted someone to do something, they said nothing to you and turned around and left? How would you deal with it? All of a sudden, there's no game to play. Then you try to reestablish a new game with someone else.

He who is in control plays the game. He who is in command knows when to leave.

The same applies to relationships with family members. Is the higher place not the place that says, "Thank you, I'm not playing this game?" One says it must be this way. Another says it must be this way. And you're sitting there saying, "Ping-pong, back and forth, back and forth." Walk away. Say, "I quit."

We assure you, the greatest gift you can give others is the opportunity to stare at their own navels and discover themselves. How can an individual truly begin to discover themselves if they are caught up playing a game? All they see is the game. They don't see themselves. Give them pause, time to reflect on themselves. You can simply say, "I quit." Who's in command then?

On the impact of seeing oneself as sufficient on the killing of another

View it from this perspective: That which they are is sufficient. They don't need more, they don't need less, that which they are is sufficient. Therefore, in their insufficiency, they are sufficient. Do you see? They are sufficient to kill. They are sufficient to hurt. They are sufficient to maim. They are sufficient to cause harm. They are sufficient to allow harm to come to themselves. If they choose to observe their sufficiency, they might choose differently. The probabilities are extremely high that they would. If they observe their sufficiency, the probabilities are extremely high that they would alter their choice. However, there is still a probability that they wouldn't. And regardless of how they observe their sufficiency, they could still make the choice to kill. For that in itself is sufficient.

View it from this perspective: An individual comes to you with a knife, intent on creating harm. Do you stand there and let him harm you? Or do you take a bigger knife and hit him first, hopefully far enough away from you that his knife won't harm you? Does that then make you insufficient? Or is that sufficient in the sense that, at that moment, you were sufficient to respond sufficiently? Do you see what we're saying here? Therefore, killing can be sufficient. Don't judge. Just observe the sufficiency.

It is sufficient to provide individuals with an opportunity to see their insufficiency. That does not mean you'd accept it. That does not mean you wouldn't change it or alter it. Sufficiency does not mean you sit at the top of a mountain and navel-gaze, we assure you. It is not a passive existence. When you perceive yourselves as sufficient, you recognize that you have the talents, the abilities and the awareness to respond to the circumstance or situation in such a manner as to create benefit.

We assure you, this concept permeates every aspect of existence. The more you observe it, the more your existence will expand. An individual who chooses to kill, chooses to do so on the basis of insufficiency. Once she observes her sufficiency, her circumstance may change, her choice would change; she may not necessarily place herself in that particular circumstance.

On seeing ourselves as sufficient as it impacts on all of society

If all the individuals in society today could see themselves as sufficient and begin to explore that, in eight generations all of society would have shifted sufficiently to see themselves as sufficient. One individual alone cannot make this change for all of society. But one individual alone can shift a great portion of society. It requires a larger group than one; it takes eight because of the empirical effect of change. In order for change to move through to the societal level, it takes eight generations.

Today in society, it's not that you think of yourselves as insufficient–you *know* yourselves as insufficient. And you're out to prove it to yourselves. We would suggest, shift. Know yourselves as sufficient, and then, dear friends, prove that to yourselves.

On the connection of the second statement to the first and to the third

The first statement, "Existence Is But an Extension of Yourself," gave you the awareness that you extend outward the illusion you create. It comes from your self. In other words, the circle on the paper is an extension of the point in the middle. It gave you the opportunity to explore the perception and the possibility. It opened you to the concept that the point did exist. As a result, it brought you to this statement, that the point is sufficient. From outward, inward; inward, outward; outward, inward. Do you see how the statements move you? One will lead you to the other. In the session on the first statement, when we suggested that existence was an extension of your self, did we not suggest that you were sufficient? We suggested it in order to lead you to this point. We assure you, dear friends, there is a reason. The reason is, you are ready. You have moved. You have grown. You have altered your existence. You've expanded yourselves to the point that now you are ready for the next step.

When you perceive yourselves as sufficient, then you will also perceive your limitlessness because there are no limits to sufficiency. Interesting, isn't it? In other words, we're not just a little bit sufficient. That's like being just a little bit pregnant. We assure you, it doesn't work. You can't say to yourself, "I am sufficient only under these circumstances," for then you are not. The statement, "I Am Sufficient," extends itself into limitlessness, which extends itself into the third statement. When you say, "I Am Sufficient," *I* is the totality that you ever were, that you are or that you ever will be, which will lead to unlimitedness.

View it from this perspective: As an ego-personality, you will observe your sufficiency on the basis of your existence. In other words, you'll see yourself for yourself: as being a sufficient dentist, a sufficient friend, a sufficient lover, a sufficient mate, a sufficient father. But now, move beyond that. Then you are sufficient for everything you've ever been, are and will be. Therefore, all past lives, present lives, future lives, are sufficient. Now, move beyond that. Then you get into soul-essence sufficiency. And move beyond that, and you uncover that your limitlessness is truly God/Goddess/The All That Is.

Now, when we speak of "manifested spirituality," we speak of your manifested spiritual health. We speak of the aspect of your spirit, of soul-essence, that you are manifesting in this existence. As you move with these statements, you expand the perception of ego-personality so that it uncovers its own interconnectedness to soul-essence. Once it moves to that perception, then, dear friends, the sky's the limit. There are no limits to how ego-personality will shift and alter to reflect soul-essence. It will still maintain a certain separateness, we assure you. But it will reflect it.

We assure you, there is no separateness between you and God/Goddess/The All That Is other than your perception. Move through using the statement, "I Am Sufficient," and you will uncover the aspects of separateness that maintain you as separate.

CHAPTER THREE

I Am Limitless; My Choices Reflect My Limitlessness

The Third Defining Statement

That which you are is without limit, and that is the end of the session.

Everything else we will say from now on will reflect that very statement. Recognize that this statement is a statement that defines your existence. If, as we're suggesting, you view it from the perspective that it is a definition of your existence, then as you begin to observe your limitlessness, so too will you observe your existence. As you observe your existence, you will observe your limitlessness. And so it goes.

"I Am Limitless." This statement is a statement that

defines all that you are. Not just ego-personalities, not just parts of ego-personalities, not just soul-essence, not physical, mental, emotional, manifested spiritual essence. It is, in fact, a statement that describes, that defines to a degree, all that you are. Use the term "define" very loosely here, for it does not define on the basis of limiting, but rather on the basis of not limiting. How can you define limitlessness? How can you describe limitlessness? There are no limits. The word definition itself is a limited perspective. Description is a limited perspective. Therefore, for us to continue to converse as we are doing now, dear friends, or to explain as we're going to do for the next hour, is to attempt to describe, define or in effect limit the aspect of limitlessness, which is that which you are.

What we will do here is provide you with the perspective that will assist you in expanding your own perspectives. This perspective will not be limitless, we assure you, for if we were to describe to you in terms the limitlessness of your limitlessness, then, dear friends, we would never speak. For no words can accurately describe limitlessness. From this perspective however, let us view your choices in existence.

View it from this perspective: A young male, approximately age thirteen, finds himself in a circumstance or situation whereby he can take a rock, throw it and break a window, or he can simply look at the rock and move on. The temptation is great. The window is a beautifully large pane of glass that reflects the Sun magnificently. It beckons to him, it calls to him, and the rock is the perfect size for his palm. He knows he has the strength and the ability to take this rock and with a certain degree of force, throw it accurately to hit the center of the pane of glass, therefore, shattering it.

At that particular point in time, he makes a choice. Regardless of the choice he makes—whether he chooses to pick up the rock and break the pane of glass or whether he chooses to view the rock, view the pane, admire both and move on—regardless of circumstance, the choice will reflect to him his perspective of his limitlessness.

In other words, he sees himself as a physical being, able and capable of a physical action with certain consequences, which will bring to him a certain physical reaction and will also affect his emotional and mental selves as well as his manifested spiritual self. That particular choice will reflect to him the perspective that he has of how unlimited a being he is. If he sees himself as limited, as being only a thirteen-year-old boy with a strong desire to break a pane of glass, then that is what he will do. If he sees himself as a thirteen-year-old boy with a strong desire to break a pane of glass but also with a desire to move beyond it, then that is also what he will do. But regardless of the choice he makes, the choice will reflect to him the perspective of his limitlessness.

The same applies to each and every one of you. Go through your existence. Observe over the last week the perspectives of your choices and how each one reflected to you your perspective of how limited or unlimited you are. When you move through a circumstance or situation, observe how you did it. Observe your emotional state, your mental state, your physical state, and observe the aspect of whether or not you felt observed, whether you allowed yourselves to interact with the circumstances in a limited fashion. You will then observe the degree to which you limit your existence.

Let's go back to that example of the young boy with the rock. In his mind, there are two choices: Take the rock and break the glass, or leave the rock and go on with his existence. That's all that he has–two choices, nothing else.

But if he perceived himself beyond that limitedness–in other words, if he saw beyond his limits–he would recognize that he has more than two choices. For example, not only could he pick up the rock and break the glass, but he could also pick up the rock and put it aside so that no one else would break the glass. Alternatively, he could pick up the rock and throw it at the glass, knowing that the rock would not break the glass. Better yet, he could pick up the rock and change it, alter it, make it into sawdust, sand or gravel–not as a result of extra strength, but strictly as a result of his perception of how he can alter his reality.

Now, this is a very finite, limited example we're using here. Let's discuss another. An individual finds him or herself in a relationship. To a degree, the relationship has a great deal of value. The other partner in the relationship is relatively easygoing, has a good sense of humor and often laughs, even at the individual's dull jokes. As a result, why not keep this individual?

Yet the perspective of the relationship is limited. In other words, what this individual sees in the relationship is that the other individual puts up with him or her and is therefore willing to accept this. It's not recognized that the other individual doesn't put up with him or her, but actually enjoys the other's company. It's not recognized that the relationship can move beyond the perspective of that which it is. Two individuals, seeing themselves and their limited perspective, spend their life sitting in front of a television screen, one with his hand down his pants, the other one filing her fingernails. That's a show that was on U.S. television not too long ago. And so they make pronouncements about life while watching television. Yet at no time is it explored that they can move beyond those limits of their reality.

When you create your reality such that that which you exist in is perceived as the total limit of your existence, then, we assure you, that is the limit to which you will live by. If you recognize, however, that you have no limits, then you will move beyond the parameters, the boundaries, the limits of your existence, and look to expand your existence.

View it from this perspective: The individual standing in a room with four walls recognizes that the four walls are the limits of his existence. If those four walls are no more than three feet away from his head, then, we assure you, he is living in a very small box. But if he pushes those walls outward, then the box becomes bigger. This concept, we assure you, is a concept that every agoraphobic goes through. Their existence is limited by their perception, and their perception is limited by their fears. Move beyond the fears, and you move beyond the perception. Move beyond the perception, and you expand the limits.

The same applies to your existence, dear friends. Every one of your fears is a wall. You can choose to leave them there. Some people, in fact, love their walls so much that they stroke them gently every day. They place their hands against them just to make sure the walls are there. They reassure themselves on a daily basis that their walls still exist, that their limits still exist. How do they do this? Through fear. They create a circumstance or situation whereby the fear is triggered over and over and over again as a methodology for them to reassure themselves that their limits in the existence they've chosen are still there. Why?

If you choose, you can limit yourselves to that wall. We would suggest, however, that you broaden the perspective such that you see that there is no wall, but that if you want to create one for the moment, you can. And then, in the next moment, you can also get rid of it. This then gives you the opportunity to recognize your limitlessness.

Notice we said that if you want to create a wall you can, and in the next moment, get rid of it. Limitlessness is not about not having fear, not building walls. Limitlessness is about knowing that you can, and choosing when to, when not to and when to remove the walls. In other words, limitlessness is about giving yourselves free choice and free will to move beyond them. To be truly limitless is to know that you can establish a limit and then remove it.

Hear the words carefully, dear friends. Because these words will assist you in moving beyond your own limits. Knowing your limitlessness is knowing that you can set limits and remove them just as easily.

Therefore, if you view your existence as a limitless being, you can say to yourselves, "Yes, this fear exists; now it is gone. Now I want it back. Now it is gone. Oh, need it again. Now it is gone. Oh, want it again. Now it is gone." And so it goes.

But in your existence, for the majority of individuals, you view your existence as a functionality of fear. A basis of fear. And the fears that you are viewing, that you are observing, are viewed as hurdles, as boundaries, as limits that must be struggled against in order to move beyond them. You fight with yourselves; you struggle with yourselves. You attempt to change your subconscious, to direct the subconscious, the conscious, the mind. You work at altering your pattern of behavior. You use therapy until you are so "therapiedout" that there's no more place for therapy. And you work and work and work and work and work–and work some more–to let go of fear.

Now, you can do that, and that has its own rewards. The rewards are that you work hard at feeling the wall. You reassure yourselves everyday that the wall is there. You touch it, you feel it, you know it. And we assure you, the harder you work at removing it, the more you know it exists. And that is the conundrum of this. The harder you work at removing a fear, the more you're reassuring yourselves that the fear exists. And so the more you then reassure yourselves that you are a limited being, that you do exist in a limited environment and that you like those limits. For after all, the more fear you have, the more you know where the walls are. And that's reassuring in and of itself. As we said, there is a benefit here.

We would suggest, however, that of greater benefit is to allow yourselves the opportunity to recognize the fear, recognize that which limits your existence, and then simply choose to get rid of it. Set it aside. Don't use it, don't apply it, don't be part of it, don't buy into it, don't set it up, don't reinforce it, don't look at it, don't struggle against it. Simply choose not to have a fear. And then you begin to observe how limitless you really are. For when you are totally limitless, you can apply fear and eliminate fear, one as quickly as the other, with no more effort experienced toward one than the other, no more energy.

Some would say that to be limitless is to define the self as having no fear. In fact, many individuals write this slogan on their cars, on their bumper stickers. No fear. Move through existence with no fear. Jump off a cliff, no fear. Jump into the jaws of a shark, no fear.

True, you can do that. But the shark will still eat you. The cliff is still high, and the landing is still rough. We would suggest that what you're then doing is attempting to convince yourselves that there are no limits or boundaries. But then at that point, you are limited by your perception that there are no limits or boundaries; therefore, you limit yourself.

That's the difficulty that most individuals have: how to become limitless and still perceive their limits. Do you deny your limits? Do you set them aside? Do you force yourselves to move in different directions so that your limits are not brought up to you, that you don't see them? After all, as the three monkeys would say, "See no evil, hear no evil, speak no evil. Therefore, there must be no evil." If you see no limits, hear no limits and speak of no limits, no limits must exist.

Quite the contrary. If you were to observe your existence, you would see how many limits you have. How many of you see yourselves as aging? That is a limit. How many of you see yourselves as capable? That is a limit. How many of you see yourselves as talented? That is a limit. How many of you see yourselves as all-enduring? That is a limit. How many of you see yourselves as being? That is a limit. How many of you see yourselves as loving? That is a limit.

And there's a good example of a limit. Most individuals, to some degree, would say to themselves, "I'm a loving person. I love this person, that person and that person. I love this dog, that cat. I love this tree, I love my new car, my new TV set, and most of all, I love the seat I'm sitting on." That is a limit.

Why not love everything regardless? In fact, why not love yourselves regardless? All of those are limits. Therefore, does limitlessness mean that you have no limits? No. It simply means that you can, if you choose, not have any.

When you are a limitless being, you can express yourself in any circumstance, in any form, in any manner, regardless of the perception. What does that mean? View it from this perspective: Over the last two years, there's been a series on television entitled *The Pretender.* It is a good television series. It talks about an individual who can pretend to be anything he wants to be, regardless of circumstance. He can be a doctor one minute, a lawyer the next, a fire chief the next, an ambulance attendant the next. He can be a surgeon, a general practitioner, a veterinarian, a judge. He can be anything he wants to be. He can even be a bum.

But the thing here is that he *pretends* to be, not that he is. To be truly limitless is to recognize that you can be all of those, regardless of circumstance, through choice. Therefore, if you want to be limitless, know that you can be a lawyer, a doctor, an ambulance attendant, a fire chief. You can be a bum, you can be a rich man, a poor man, an Indian chief. You can be anything you would like to be, not just pretend, but be. That is your limitlessness.

When you see yourselves as "just" this type of person or that type of person—"I'm just a wife; I'm just a husband; I am just a lover; I am just an accountant; I am just a lawyer; I am just a secretary"—we assure you, just as you are "just," you are also limited.

But know that you can be any of those and still change; then you become limitless. The key to limitlessness is to recognize that you have the choice to change. Let us repeat this. *The key to your limitlessness is for you to recognize that you have the choice to change.* That's your choice. You can choose to remain as that which you are, or you can choose to change. When you know that you have that choice—that you can make that choice and that you give yourselves the freedom to choose to remain or to change—then, dear friends, you become limitless beings. For then nothing, absolutely nothing, will define your existence. Not even the definition that you choose to change. Nothing will define you. Nothing will limit you. Nothing will set boundaries for you.

Now, does this mean that in a society where you are limitless, you would not follow the rules of that society? Absolutely not. You might choose to do so. You might also choose not to do so. That is your choice. You have the freedom to choose, to change, to alter.

Therefore, if you find yourselves in a circumstance that is unacceptable to the self, choose to change the circumstance. If you find yourselves in relationships that are unacceptable to the self, choose to change the circumstance. If you find yourselves in jobs that are unacceptable to you, choose to change the circumstance. If you find yourselves listening to words that are unacceptable to you, choose to change the circumstance. If you find yourselves doing things that are no longer acceptable to you, choose to change the circumstance.

The message here is easy. Give yourselves the freedom to alter and shift your existence at will, and you become limitless. Most people don't. Most people spend months–years, sometimes–justifying to themselves why one choice is being made. They justify to themselves why they have to change jobs, change life partners change clothes–why they have to go out and buy clothes. They justify to themselves and to those around them the choices of their existence. The more time you spend justifying, the more you can observe your limits and the less you will observe your limitlessness.

But to observe your limitlessness, you might as well observe your limits. For one is as intrinsic to the other as the other is to the one. They're tied together. If you want to observe how limitless you are, observe how limited you are. You will be amazed, we assure you. How many of you give yourselves the freedom to change your choice in the moment as you choose? Not many, we assure you.

Can you? Yes. You are limitless beings. Each choice you make will reflect that. The amount of justification you give to yourselves to make that choice reflects that. An individual who, on a continuous basis, spends three minutes justifying his choices, has fewer limits than an individual who spends three days, three weeks, three months, three years doing the same.

And you laugh sometimes. We do hear your laughter, dear friends, with regards to "three years." But we assure you, how many individuals change cars on a day-by-day basis? None, other than the fellow who's renting one. Most individuals, when they buy a car, hang on to it. They keep it. They love it, they nourish it, they cherish it, or they treat it like a piece of dirt. But regardless of how they treat it, they don't give themselves permission to change it. When the car starts acting up, doing something crazy, do they give themselves permission to change it? Not at all. Better to go fix it and keep it, rather than change it.

Take a look at your house. How many individuals buy a house and stay there, regardless of how the neighborhood goes, who the neighbors are? Regardless of circumstance—how the air quality is, how the quality of life is—they still stay there. Why? Because they bought it, and they will live in it, and they will die in it. And true, they will, instead of simply saying, "This is no longer acceptable to me. I choose to change. This is a limit that I had that I no longer have. Let's expand, let's grow, let's alter, let's shift."

How many individuals begin the process of observing themselves in such a way that they begin to discover all of their limits? When you observe yourselves, dear friends, you will observe your limits.

Change the word *limits* to *fears*. Perhaps that will have more resonance with you. Fears are that which create limits in your existence. If you fear something, you will stop yourselves from exploring, from moving in that direction. Take the example of the individual who fears skiing, who cannot ski, who sees himself as unable to ski, who fears the concept of skiing. Would he ever approach a mountain? Not likely. And if he did, we assure you, there would be no snow on it. Would he ever go on a ski lift? Not likely. "The weather's too cold, it's too damp, it's too humid, it's too high. I don't like heights, I don't like going on a rope up a hill. I don't like skis, I don't like wood slats. What are poles for? I don't like these clothes." The individual will come up with every excuse you could think of to stop himself from skiing.

Why? Because he fears skiing. And is that the only aspect of his life affected by it? No. Because he fears skiing, he fears many other things. He fears the uncontrollable, for to a degree, skiing is truly an uncontrollable experience. True, you can go down the hill pretty fast and you can, through technique and ability, control your descent reasonably well. But what if you can't?

What if you don't have the talent and ability? What if you don't know how to ski? What if you can't control your descent? What would occur? You'd go down that hill so fast, you'd end up having drinks at the bottom before everybody else got off the top. And you might even hurt yourself in the process. That would be an uncontrollable experience.

As a result, you never allow yourself to explore. Your fear of skiing will affect your existence. In other words, when an opportunity comes that demands or requires of you a certain willingness to explore, you won't. Why? Because you fear skiing, and that fear is carried over into other circumstances. And so your existence becomes more limited.

But if you set that fear aside and say, "I choose not to have it. I choose not to explore it. I don't need it, don't want it. Thank you, good-bye." Then at that point, you give yourself the opportunity to explore other aspects of your existence. You might never go up a ski hill—especially if you live in the desert; that would be difficult. But you would give yourself an opportunity to explore new aspects of your existence, new areas of your life, new directions such that you would find yourself moving beyond the aspect of your existence.

Witness the rain that's coming down right now. An uncontrollable aspect affecting this particular recording, is it not, dear Maggie? And you have been concerned about it, have you not? Everyone here is looking at the rain, thinking about the rain, wondering about it, distracted by it. Why? You chose this rain, dear friends. You attracted it. Enjoy it. It is not a limit. It is only a limit if you make it a limit. So there is the pitter-patter of raindrops on the recording, dear Maggie. As one would say, "Who cares?" Another might interpret the pitter-patter as the pitter-patter of a thousand little feet in the background. Perception, that is all it is. The perception that the noise will affect the quality of the recording limits the enjoyment of the recording, limits the enjoyment of the words.

And now it's stopped. Interesting, isn't it?

The more you expand your consciousness of that which you yourselves fear, the more you will discover your limitlessness. Let's take this example of the rain. Dear Maggie, please indulge us, if you don't mind? There was fear within yourself in regards to the quality of the recording, was there not? To all those here this evening, some of you were very distracted and some were slightly distracted, but all of you had moments of distraction, true? And why? What did you fear hearing and listening to? That you are limitless beings? That you can choose to move beyond your limits? The fears that you have experienced describe your limits. When you fear something, you allow it to interfere in the pleasure, enjoyment and expansion of your existence.

How many of you sat there in total amazement and wonderment and simply enjoyed the sound that the raindrops made? Not one. Interesting! We did. Did it affect our conversation, dear friends? Did it limit our expression? In fact, it expanded it. We used it as an example to expand the consciousness as we are discussing the aspect of limitlessness. We were not limited by it. We did not fear it. And as a result, it became useful fodder for the information we are trying to present to you.

Fascinating how easy that was, wasn't it? You too can create your existence in this fashion. You too can live on a daily basis in the same way that we experienced the rain. When you find yourselves in a line at the grocery store with the woman in front having no change whatsoever, looking through her purse, the kid behind you screaming his head off because his mother will not let him have the chocolate bar that is sitting right beside him, and the man behind her impatient and sighing at the top of his breath—don't get upset, frustrated, reactive to that energy. Instead, enjoy it. See the pleasure in it, the wonderment of it. Appreciate how wonderful it was for the woman in front to give everyone behind her an opportunity to experience their limits. She did that beautifully. How many individuals would be able to go through their purse forty times and never find the right amount of change? It takes talent, it takes ability, it takes creativeness. Observe it and enjoy it.

And the child behind you who is screaming his head off because he doesn't get the chocolate bar that he wants and his mother is getting angry—enjoy that interaction too. You don't have to let it affect you; you simply have to observe it. It is part of your creative experience. It is part of the room that you find yourselves in. But you don't have to stay in the room. If you find yourselves in those circumstances, and you find that this is unacceptable to you, why not simply leave? True, you won't get the products you had intended to buy. But as we said earlier, "Who cares?" You can buy them two minutes from now or ten minutes from then. You can buy them the next day. You can buy them at any other time. You can simply shift lanes. You can go to another store. But every time you sit there and say to yourselves, "I must stay in this line. I have no time, no place, no space. I must get these things, this is what I must do," then you limit yourselves.

Why would you say that? Because you fear being without those limits. You love to know where your walls are. Therefore, when you find yourselves getting frustrated by circumstance in existence, know, dear friends, that you are touching the wall to know exactly where it is. Know it with a passion. For we assure you, the more frustrated you get, the more you want to know how solid that wall is—just in case you have to lean against it.

But what if you found out that there was no wall? Or that the wall is really made of water? That when you put your hand against it, you can simply move through it, simply flow through it? Then we assure you, as fast as you got frustrated in that line, you would build another wall even more solid, rather than simply saying, "This is acceptable, let's explore this. Let's move to change."

Here's a good story, and this happened approximately ten minutes ago. There is a restaurant in this city not too far from our present location. There is an individual who sat down, and the waitress brought him the menu and a knife. She didn't bring napkins or a fork. This individual was so upset that he has berated the waitress beyond belief because he did not get a fork and a napkin, only the knife. Not that she wasn't going to get it for him, but that it wasn't prepared for him. His existence was being challenged. He likes to go into the restaurant and have everything prepared exactly the same every time. This waitress knows him—he's a regular customer and she knew this—but she forgot. Why did she forget? Because she was attempting to push her limits, and as a result, she tried to push his instead.

There are many, many individuals who do the same thing: the man who wakes up in the morning and finds he has no socks in his sock drawer and gets upset at his wife because the laundry wasn't done; the housewife who comes home at night and finds that the children have played at homemaking, and the kitchen is completely covered in food. And we do mean covered in food—floors, walls, ceilings. Why? Because the child had a good time pretending to be Mommy, cooking. And Mommy gets upset.

Or what about the housewife who comes home and dinner isn't ready when her husband's been there all day, and she gets upset. Or the husband comes home, dinner's not ready, and because the housewife's been there all day, he gets upset. You go to work and you find yourself without your coffee in the morning because the coffee shop is closed down. Someone is sick. You get upset—little things, big things. The report isn't on your desk when you wanted it. The coworker didn't do her part, and you become responsible. Someone imposes her will on your existence, and you react.

All of these are circumstances about which—because of your psychology, because of your belief that you are limited beings—you think in limited terms. In other words, that which was is that which is and is that which will be. And as a result, you don't allow yourselves to change. You don't move with the circumstances that are presented to you. You attempt to maintain your existence in the same direction all the time.

We did a series entitled "Control vs. Command." Control is what we are speaking of here. Every aspect of your existence that you maintain is an aspect of control. When you force circumstances to be a certain way in order to satisfy your perspective of your existence as limited beings, you are controlling the circumstances of your existence.

To move to a perspective of command, you must observe yourselves as limitless beings. This is because limitless beings simply move with the circumstances they find themselves in and give themselves permission to choose to change. Therefore, when the report is not on the desk at a certain time, so what? Go do something else. It'll be there three minutes from now. And so it goes.

With this statement, "I Am Limitless; My Choices Reflect My Limitlessness," we've explored with you how your choices reflect your limitlessness. The fewer choices you give yourselves the freedom to make, the less limitless you are and the more limited you are. The greater freedom you give yourselves to choose, the more you express your limitlessness.

Observe your choices. Observe the degree of justification for your choices, and you will observe how limited an existence you enjoy. And we assure you, you enjoy it. For if you did not enjoy it, you would change it.

Therefore, when you see yourselves in a circumstance that is repetitive in your existence, regardless of what it is—whether it be getting up in the morning, putting your pants on left leg first and right leg next, shaving, getting dressed, going to work, coming home, or whether it be being in the same type of relationships over and over and over again, or smoking the same cigarette every three minutes—each one of those choices reflects your limitlessness.

When you do something repetitively over and over and over again, we assure you, you are simply advising yourselves how limited your existence is. Observe it. A cigarette smoker is a perfect example of someone who is very limited. Why? Because there is a need to smoke one every so often. It's a repetitive action.

We assure you, if you begin to observe your existence, to observe only those aspects that are repetitive in your existence, you will be amazed at how many of your actions are repetitive on a minute-by-minute, hour-by-hour and day-by-day basis–and we haven't even discussed week-by-week, month-by-month and year-by-year here. If we were to discuss those, they would be infinite.

Begin to observe yourselves. We assure you, dear friends, observe your choices and discover your limitlessness. If you meditate on it, this statement that we've given you will bring about to you an opportunity to explore your existence. That's all it will do. It won't change your existence. It won't alter your existence. It won't make you change. What it will do is give you the opportunity to explore your existence. And an exploration is without limits, for it is unknown.

Have you ever gone on a trip into the forest? You don't know what's on the other side, and you certainly don't know what's in between. You know that you're going to get to the other side, but you don't know how. The same applies to your existence. You know where you stand. You don't know where you're going, and you certainly don't know how you're going to get there. But what an exploration, what a journey. We assure you, it is a valuable journey. For in that journey, you will discover that you, dear friends, are all limitless beings.

Limitlessness–what a fun way to live! Give yourselves the chance to have fun, play, laugh and experience joy. You can't limit laughter. Have you ever tried? Have you ever tried to stop yourselves from laughing in the middle of a good laugh? Impossible. You can control it to a degree, but you cannot stop it. Laugh. The more you bring humor in your existence, the more limitlessness you expand on.

I am a limitless being, or "I Am Limitless; My Choices Reflect My Limitlessness." It could be said, "I'm a funny guy, let me laugh."

Additional Comments

On how a state of "beingness" is a limitation

View it from this perspective: On many occasions, both individually and as a group, we ourselves have suggested to you that to move from a state of doingness to a state of beingness has benefit and value. But even a state of beingness, in and of itself, has certain limits, for a state of beingness is definable; it has a definition. And as a result, it is limited.

Do not view our statement as being negative, or as a reduction of the self. Being talented, for example, is a benefit. It has value to the self. Yet being talented is still limited; it has a limit. Talents, in and of themselves, are based on perspectives of creation: The fact that you are created as an ego-personality and that you are therefore a talented ego-personality is a limit in and of itself. If you were a soul-essence with talents, that too would also be a limit, for you see yourself as being talented.

Whether you see yourselves as being talented or not being talented—regardless of circumstance—it is limiting in that you then define yourselves. When you define yourselves, you limit yourselves. We would suggest that a greater perspective is simply to apply whatever talents you have in the moment to the circumstance as it occurs, regardless of circumstance or existence. And therefore, being talented is irrelevant. The more you define yourselves, the more you limit yourselves.

The session we gave you entitled "Two Steps to Go" (*Sedona Journal of Emergence!*, February, 2001) was, to a degree, a limit, but it was an appreciable limit. It was something that would still expand your existence. When we suggested that you observe yourselves such that you begin to appreciate yourselves, recognize that that particular recording was made, at that point, with the intent to bring about a shift in consciousness through a certain step-by-step process. We defined the steps. There's that word defined again. As a result, yes, the ten-step program we suggested to you is a limited perspective, we assure you. It has its limits; it has its boundaries. But it has validity, in and of itself; it will expand your existence. Once you achieve a perspective of expansion, then you move beyond the necessity to apply that ten-step program. And at that point, dear friends, you then have a perspective that is far more limitless.

Now from that perspective, if you perceive yourself and your talents, if you observe yourself and your talents and abilities, then, yes, you observe them. You can even define yourself by your talents and abilities. Some people do. Some people see themselves as great tennis players, great piano players, great artists, and that's how they define themselves. We would suggest, recognize that they only form a part of that which you are–that part of which you can, if you choose, apply in the moment as circumstances exist. If you define yourself as being talented, then you see yourself only on the basis of talents. You don't see yourself beyond that. If you define yourself as being loving, you see yourself only as loving, and you don't move beyond that. That, in and of itself, is a limiting factor. Being loving is a broad, expansive perspective that–if you were to observe it and apply it in your existence–would move far beyond what others around you already manifest in their existence. You would even move beyond the Nazarene, were you to be completely into loving. But even that would have its limits. It would be a broad, expansive perspective, but it would still be limited, for it is limited on the basis of your reality–on how you perceive being loving.

If you see yourself as being talented, would you see yourself with all of your talents and abilities? Or would you see yourself only with certain talents and abilities and apply those? Therefore, that is a limited perspective. If you broadened that perspective and saw that you had unlimited talents and abilities, then you wouldn't see yourself as being talented. You would simply see yourself as being, and even that would be a limit. For to observe yourself beyond that is to observe yourself as simply existing. We use the term "being" here because there is no other term in the English language that would define the concept we are suggesting here. As we said at the beginning of this session, the English language is very limiting. We suggested that the statement, "I Am Limitless," was the end of the session; we could not expand on that. Our attempt to expand on it created limits. You cannot expand on limitlessness. It is without limits.

The statement, "I Am Limitless," also goes along with "My Choices Reflect My Limitlessness"—both together. The first has value, in and of itself. It is a defining statement; it does not need to be expanded on. We added "My Choices Reflect My Limitlessness," because we wanted to give you a perspective of how to define yourselves such that you could move to the perspective of limitlessness. That is why we gave the second part of that statement. The first was more than enough, dear friends, we assure you.

On what lies beyond being loving

View it from this perspective: That which is simply is. That which lies beyond being loving is loving—love itself. Being loving is applying; loving is simply being. Interesting, isn't it? You become, you manifest, you are that which is, as opposed to simply being that. The difficulty here is in the term "being" because of the limitation of the English language. We assure you, if you were to view the term "being loving" as a state of loving, that state itself is limiting. But when you are love, there is no limit.

On dying as a means of understanding our limitlessness

Dying wouldn't serve as a means of understanding your limitlessness in third-dimensional reality. First, recognize that when you chose to incarnate as soul-essence, you did not fully appreciate your limitlessness. If you did, you would be God/Goddess/The All That Is. As a soul-essence, you have certain degrees of separation from God/Goddess/The All That Is. Those degrees of separation are limits. Therefore, to appreciate your limitlessness, you must experience limits. As soul-essence, you do, but the experience is not as intense as when you incarnate in this third-dimensional reality, which is a very limited reality of existence. As a result, you choose to incarnate so as to experience, in a moment of intensity, a certain intensity as to limits in order to observe your limitlessness within yourselves.

Now, as ego-personality incarnated, if you were simply to cast off feet of clay, then you would go through the process of reintegration and reevaluation with soul-essence and become one with soul-essence. And you would, to a degree, experience a certain aspect of limitlessness. But you would not experience that limitlessness in a conscious fashion.

The statement, "I Am Limitless; My Choices Reflect My Limitlessness," is designed to broaden your perspective of existence in such a way that you expand your choices in existence to bring about a greater awareness, a greater enlightenment of your own consciousness. This can then broaden the experience of soul-essence and therefore, broaden soul-essence to the perspective of becoming one with God/Goddess/The All That Is. It's all inter-linked, dear friends. That which you do is that which they do. The next statement, "That Which You Are Is That Which I Am, and That Which I Am Is That Which You Are," is exactly what we're talking about here.

You come to experience in order to appreciate that which you are. And in appreciating that which you are, you can then allow yourselves to be that which you are.

On a technique for creating energy

It's a very difficult technique, dear friends. This technique will take you a long time to learn. In fact, it is so difficult that it might even be beyond your talents and abilities. It might be beyond your perception of your limitlessness. The technique is so difficult that we will show it to you, and you will not understand it.

Here is a creation of energy. There it went.

Notice the effect? All of you laughed. Notice the energy? It was created; you responded. Notice the technique? It was very intense, we assure you. We used certain methodologies that we have difficulty describing. However, creation is simply that—creation. We're being tongue-in-cheek here, dear friends. But recognize, there is no technique to creation. Simply create, which is another way of saying simply choose. Fascinating, isn't it? The more you explore how to define the aspect of limitlessness, the more you explore how you define your limits.

On being anything we choose to be

You can choose to be a doctor and study. That is one methodology. If your perspective of being a doctor is that you must go through four years of university, six years of medical school and four years of internship in order to become a doctor, then by all means, go ahead and do so.

However, you can be a doctor quite easily. If your perspective is that your society's rules apply to your existence and that you must therefore live within those rules, then you will manifest an existence based on society's rules. However, if your perspective is different—simply that you can be a doctor and therefore, you are—then we assure you, you will be. The knowledge that you need exists within yourselves. If you choose, you can use that knowledge; or you can go and read books and gain knowledge; or you can go to school and gain knowledge; or you can go and apply yourselves and gain knowledge. The choice is yours. The methodology is part of the limit of your perspective.

Recognize that we said your choices reflect your limitlessness. If you choose to perceive your existence as having to follow a certain pattern, dear friends, then that again is a reflection of your perception of limitlessness, isn't it? The statement was simply, "Your Choices Reflect Your Limitlessness." Therefore, what would you like to choose?

If you choose to simply be—because the knowledge exists within yourselves, you're aware of that, and you are—then patients will come to you. Others will come to you for assistance. You will be a doctor. However, you will not have that little piece of paper on the wall that says you're a practicing M.D. Now, is that little piece of paper important to you? If it is, then that choice reflects the degree of limitlessness that you apply in your existence.

There's no right or wrong here. This isn't about denigration or expansion of the self. It's simply a statement: "Your choices reflect your limitlessness." Therefore, if you choose to go to school, that is one reflection. If you choose to learn from books, that is another reflection. If you choose to learn through applying your knowledge, that is another reflection. If you choose to simply know, that is another reflection. All are just as valid as the others. They are all choices.

Interesting, isn't it? All of you, dear friends, are intent on limiting your perspective of limitlessness by defining your choices; they must fit a certain parameter of existence. Why? What we're suggesting here is that you can change the parameters of your existence.

You'll say to yourselves, "But we live in a third-dimensional reality with certain third-dimensional limitations." True. But who says you have to stay here? Why not choose to be in different dimensions simultaneously? Nice concept, yes? You won't let yourselves do that because you are a third-dimensional entity. But the answer is, why not? Nothing is stopping you except your choices—except yourselves. Nobody said you had to keep playing this game. If you choose to, then that choice reflects your limitlessness. Now, that isn't to say that this is right or wrong, good or bad, but that your choices are what are limiting you. Fascinating, isn't it?

We're not saying here, "Become limitless beings." We're saying, "You *are* limitless beings." And the choices you make simply reflect that; they reflect your perspective of your limitlessness. Therefore, we gave you the statement, "I Am Limitless; My Choices Reflect My Limitlessness." One part says, "I have no limits"; the other part says, "But I do."

On the "complexity" of making choices that affect others

It's complex because you make it complex, dear friends. You are attached to the results of your choices. You're attached from the perspective of your perception of your responsibility, from your perspective of action and reaction, from your perspective of co-creation, from your perspective of codependency. Each of these are limits you impose on yourself. You can, if you choose, do so. That is your choice. But you can also choose not to. If your existence is based on the choice that these aspects must define your existence, then they will. As a result, you will define your limits and your limitlessness.

However, move beyond those aspects–don't define yourselves, don't choose the must–and then you expand your limitlessness. For example, what would happen if you're in an organization and it's your responsibility, as chief financial officer, to make a choice with regards to the funding of the organization. Certain loans, certain financial arrangements, must be made. And if you don't make these certain financial arrangements, the company will fold. If you do make these financial arrangements, there is a probability that the company will not fold and possibly expand.

If you fold, a number of individuals are tossed out of work–families are affected, children are affected, the children's education, the economy is affected because now there are fewer jobs. Each of those factors should be taken into consideration. If you don't fold, then all is supported–the jobs, the businesses around you. The little guy down the street selling hot dogs is happy because now he still has his customers around. All of these things should also be taken into account.

Now from your perspective, you're suggesting that each of those aspects must be considered for the choice to be made. And as a result, as a responsible individual, you would consider all of those aspects before making your choice. You would sit, and you would ponder each of those to make an informed choice, a choice that would bring about what you perceive as the greatest benefit to all concerned.

But the driving force is not the choice to bring about the greatest benefit to all concerned. The driving force is what will make you survive. Your job? Your company? For without your company, you have no job. With no job, you have no way of defining yourself. You're no longer part of an organization, you're no longer part of a whole.

So the driving force for your choice, really, is not to ensure the survival of a company, because you yourself would not leave it the moment you made the choice. But the driving force is rather to ensure your survival within the confines of the company. As a result, you spend a great deal of time justifying to yourself the reason for your choice. What you're not perceiving is your fear–your fear of not being with a job, of not having a way of defining yourself, of not being part of a whole. As a result, you look at yourself in the position of chief financial officer, and you spend a great deal of time looking at this situation, pondering the alternatives, looking at the possibilities and therefore making, as you call it, an informed choice.

But what if you simply chose? What if, just like those other individuals, you tossed a coin in the air: heads you fold, tails you go for it. What would happen? Then the next step would be, if it comes up heads, "Oh dear, must close the doors. Better lock them now." If it comes up tails, "Oh dear, must keep going. Better go to the bank immediately."

And so each choice would lead you to another choice, regardless of which choice you make. And we do say this: Regardless of which choice you make, whether it be an informed choice or not, the aspect of your own survival will still be considered and will still affect the choice you make.

Your fears, your personal fears–fears about who you are, how you define yourself, how you interact with others–will define your choice, regardless of your position in a large corporation or not. As a result, this isn't about anything else. This isn't about cocreation, codependency, coexistence. This isn't about responsibility. This isn't about a large number of individuals being dependent on you and responsible to you. This is about you and your fears. And in the end, the energy of choice is simply to choose. Either way, you will ensure your survival.

As to the energy of choice, once you give yourselves that freedom to recognize that the choice can simply be a choice, and move in one direction or the other, who's to say that if you chose to close the doors, somebody wouldn't come along and open them after you? Who's to say that if you chose to go to the bank to get financing, you wouldn't lose all the financing within twenty-four hours? There are no guarantees. What you're looking to do is to control all the aspects of existence to ensure that your choices are valid. And you fail to perceive that regardless of the choice, it is valid.

The choices you make reflect your limitlessness. We assure you, when you get caught up in the circumstances of a large corporation–the responsibility, the authority, the codependency and the cocreation aspects–you are reflecting back to yourselves your limitlessness and the degree of limitlessness that you allow in your existence. To choose is simply to choose, no more and no less. The fear that you have is, if you choose to close the doors, then you will be out of a job. And as a result, you work diligently not to.

Your choices are reflections of your own limitlessness. It doesn't matter how you want to justify it, how you want to describe it, how you want to define it, they do reflect that portion of your limitlessness. This is not an oversimplification, we assure you. Existence is simple, dear friends. There is no complication to existence. It is the mind that likes to complicate it–"you must do this, you must do that"; "you should do this, you should that"; "you ought to do this, you ought to do that." And so what you do is set and establish limits and boundaries for yourselves.

Every time you use those words, observe yourselves, dear friends–you'll observe the limits and the boundaries you establish for yourselves. Set aside the words; stop using the words. Recognize that you are limitless, and then start making choices on the basis of your limitlessness, not on the basis of your limits.

View it from this perspective: If you were to take our example that, if that chief financial officer simply chose not to go to the bank, does that mean the company will fold? It's a probability, yes. A high degree of probability. But there's also a degree of probability that it won't. And if it does, what would be the worst thing that could happen? People will be out of work for a period of time, true. But they will find other work, and everything else will still function.

It's like the individual who sits in a company and sees himself as being indispensable and refuses to take a vacation because, after all, the company cannot do without him. And when he goes on vacation, everything goes to hodgepodge and a mess, and he has to come back and fix everything that happened while he was away. That individual is convincing himself that the company cannot function without him. If he is fired, if he leaves, if he dies, we assure you, the company will continue. The universe will continue to exist whether you choose based on your limits or on your limitlessness. It will continue.

And the beauty of the universe is that everything is in perfect order. Nothing is out of place. Therefore, whether you choose through your limits or whether you choose without your limits, the choices have the same validity and the universe will function. Therefore, why not choose without limits?

Recognize that the choice is always yours, dear friends. However, if you have the choice of a rowboat or of a twenty-foot yacht with a bar, a TV set and a stereo system with surround-sound, and all you need to do is cross your swimming pool, we would suggest that you take the yacht. It's a lot more fun.

On goal-oriented choices versus the serendipitous kind

We would suggest that both goal-oriented choices and serendipitous ones have the same validity. View it from this perspective: When you make a choice with intent, you are trying to direct the choice. In other words, "I want to go here, so every choice I make will take me there. And specifically, this choice must take me there." But what if all you do is set direction for yourself, "I'd like to go there," and then, knowing that your choices will take you there, you simply choose? The intent is not to go there–you will get there, that is your direction. But who cares when you get there or how you get there? You'll get there.

Now, when you limit your choice on the basis of direction or intent, as you suggested, that choice is just as valid as when you choose to go serendipitously in the moment. Neither one is more valid than the other; it is simply that you make a different choice. What we're suggesting here is that when you make the choice with intent, observe your limits. When you make the choice without intent, observe your limits. And then choose which one you'd like to do.

This isn't about judgment–you're adding judgment to your choice. This is simply about choosing. Make a choice and go with it. If you don't like it, change it. If you don't like that one, change it again. If you like that one, stick with it. If you don't like it again, change it again. If you like it for a while, stick with it. When it gets to the end of the while, change it again. The point is that you give yourselves permission to choose to change or to choose to stay. In other words, you give yourselves permission to change, to alter, to shift your existence. And once you do that, then you become that limitless being. You manifest yourselves as the limitless beings that you are. For a limitless being does not set limits; it simply chooses.

All of you are attempting to define yourselves on the basis of your limited perspective of morality, of spirituality. You're trying to define on the basis of acceptability to yourselves; each choice must be acceptable to the self. Who says so? Why can't you choose something that's unacceptable to the self? Why can't you choose something that's unacceptable to another? True, choice will lead you in a certain direction, but once you're in that direction, you can always choose to change.

Now, some would say, if you choose a life of crime, if you choose to steal, that choice will lead you to jail. And once you're in jail, it's very hard to change to get out of jail. You don't have one of those little cards that a certain board game gives you. No get-out-of-jail-free cards. However, we would suggest that, yes, once you're in jail, you're in jail for your period of time, but you don't have to choose to go back. You don't have to choose to continue to steal. You don't have to choose to continue your existence. You've experienced jail, thank you, didn't like it, left it. Do you see? Or you can say, "I experienced jail. I loved it a lot, I want to go back." Each choice is just a valid as the other. You're adding judgment to your choices. Stop adding judgment. Yes, the choices will lead you in a certain direction. Can you change that direction? Yes.

If you've stolen a number of times and you've been caught and are going to jail, then at that point, the only opportunity you'll have to change is once you're in jail. You can choose to change, you don't have to be in jail. Jail is a perspective. You can be very free in jail, we assure you. It has often been said, who is the most jailed person: the one inside the cell, or the one outside making sure you stay inside?

We assure you, freedom is a perspective. It doesn't

have to be physical. Therefore, many choices can be made. But you limit yourselves. You see yourselves as going to jail, and therefore, you have no freedom. The bird in the cage often has more freedom than you would know. Sure, it can't fly around. It can't go around the room in the air, but it does have a certain degree of freedom. You just need to perceive it, to see it. Change your perception, and you change your choices. Change your choices, and you change your existence. The person in jail who recognizes the value of freedom will change his choices. And as a result, you won't get a get-out-of-jail-free card, but in the Canadian system, you'll get out in two or three months, which is almost as good.

Choose to your greater benefit. Choose to your benefit. Choose to no benefit or to your lesser benefit. Regardless, they are all valid.

Look at it this way: If you decide to go to school, it will take a period of time. That particular choice will lead you in a certain direction. Once you get into school and you find you don't like your courses, why not leave? Change. Go to another course. Who says that you can't go into this class or that class? The rules say? Excuse us for laughing slightly here, but as we understand it, at no time in any educational institution do they place guards with big baseball bats and large guns by the door to ensure that only those students who are signed up can go into the class. In fact, you can even go into an educational institution where you're not even signed up.

What's to stop you from attending a university class now? You fear it. You would walk in, you would be fearful, and somebody would say to you, "You don't belong here, you're too fearful. Leave." But if you walked in with a robe over you, a cap on your head, glasses and books in your hand, they'd say, "Excuse me, Professor, this is your class." Why not? All it takes is a robe and a cap.

View it from this perspective: You can choose to be a psychiatrist; all it takes is a chair and a couch. You can choose to be a lawyer; all it takes is the will to talk and the ability to lie. We assure you, this is not for fun. The one thing lawyers are good at is lying. Why? Because they are attempting to convince others that what they do has validity. To a degree it does, but the majority of time it doesn't. But they're good at convincing. The same applies to politicians. Why is it that you cannot sue a politician in the country of Canada? Because it is known that politicians lie. Therefore, because you know that a politician lies, you cannot sue him for lying. That is a fact, we assure you. There is a ruling in the Supreme Court of Canada that you cannot sue a politician for lying because politicians, by their very nature, are liars. And the same could be said about a number of other professions, we assure you.

However, the key here is that you can be anything you want to be, do anything you want to do–simply choose. You want to be a professor? Go to school, stand in front of the class and say to everybody, "Yes, I am here today to teach you." Security will only come to turn you out because you fear it.

On the part of you that is making the choice

Every part of you makes choices. All of you. Your ego-personality makes choices. Ego-personality can be defined as the physical, mental, emotional and manifested spiritual essence. As a result, ego-personality makes choices. Soul-essence makes choices. Each part within your ego-personality has free will and free choice—they choose too. You could call it synchronicity, in a way, or you could call it a good commune inside you, all choosing at the same time.

View it from this perspective: The ego-personality, as it's created, is created as a whole. But as it continues through its existence, it expands itself by creating parts of itself, very similar to that which you perceive to be the God/Goddess/The All That Is expansion to soul-essence. Each part has its own free will and free choice. Therefore, each part makes choices. Often, some parts choose one thing and other parts choose another on the basis of their creative energy. This is why sometimes you feel the push-pull going on inside of you, and you wonder why you never move. It's because some parts are pulling this way and some are pulling that way. People who sabotage themselves—who say, "But I want to do this," and then they sabotage themselves—

it's because one part says yes and the other part says yes to something else.

So each part then is created with its own perspective. As a result of this, it requires a certain degree of willingness on a number of parts to make a choice. In other words, all the energy, all the parts or all the selves in the foot, must all work together in order to move the foot forward.

We would suggest, however, that you go beyond synchronicity to collectivity—such as a collective consciousness. View the collective consciousness of that which we are. In effect, you could understand that which we are by understanding your own cellular structure and how it all moves together, or you could understand on the basis of your ego-personality parts. As a result, all must choose. Some choose one way, some choose the other way. If there's a majority of choice one way, then everything moves that way.

On the role judgment plays in making choices

Judgment comes in because there's a number of parts within you that sit there and say, "But, oh dear, what about this, what about that? I need this circumstance; I need that circumstance. This isn't in action, this isn't in place, this must be in place." And so it goes around and around. The mind gets caught up with this and continues the game. And as a result, you begin justifying to yourselves the reason why a certain choice must be made. So you spend a great portion of your energy, and a great portion of your existence, justifying the choices you make to yourselves.

View it from this perspective: In an average life span of 73.9 years, the average person living 73.9 years will have spent 71.4 years justifying choices and the rest of the time choosing. That's the amount of energy they expend. If you take 73.9 years on the basis of energy, 71.4 years would be energy spent justifying their choices and the remainder just the energy spent choosing. Interesting, isn't it?

Now, think about this: If you spent 70 years justifying, that's 1.4 years more of choosing. Think of how many more choices you can make over that 1.4 years. Then expand beyond that. But give yourself an out—keep at least two years of justification for yourselves.

On being rational when it comes to making choices

You think you have to make rational choices because you see yourselves as rational beings. But are you? May we suggest that there's something you do that's very irrational? May we suggest here that the most irrational thing you ever did was to talk to a disembodied entity speaking through someone else's body. That has to be one of the most irrational things you've ever done. And we assure you, if others were to look at you on that basis, the men in little white coats would come and get you. But you see it as rational.

Rational is a perspective. That you choose to view your existence on the basis of rationality is a perspective. That you choose to view your decisions on the basis on rationalization is a perspective. It has validity—it has no more or less validity than that which we suggest to you. It is your choice. However, we would suggest, don't get caught up with the perspective that you are a rational individual. We assure you, you're the most irrational individual in this whole group. But then again, so are the others. We said "most irrational," but then most irrational could be used to define all of the others in this group.

Think of it from this perspective: What would others say if they could look in on this group [attending the session]? A bunch of individuals, gathered around a table, talking into a microphone, speaking to some idiot lying in a chair, his eyes closed, his mouth flapping, and nobody is willing to say anything. They don't know whether to speak or not speak. They're asking questions that they're not sure of. They're getting answers that make them think, but beyond that, it's not doing a whole lot more. They're being titillated every now and again. They laugh, they cry, and in the meantime, the others looking through the window at this group are thinking, "What a bunch of crazy kooks!"

We assure you, as a group, you're very irrational, dear friends. Not many individuals would speak to someone whose eyes are closed and whose mouth is flapping and whose hands are moving like crazy. From your perspective, this is completely rational, isn't it? But view it from the perspective that we've suggested: that which you see as rational, others would see as irrational. Therefore, don't define yourselves on the basis of your rationality. Give yourselves permission to look beyond it.

As the statement says, "The Choices I Make Reflect My Limitlessness." It doesn't say, the choices The Wonders make, the choices he or she makes. It says, the choices *I* make. When you're saying to yourselves, "I Am Limitless; the Choices I Make Reflect My Limitlessness," it's the choices you make, not anyone else.

And when you are sufficient, dear friends, you also recognize that being limited is acceptable. But being limitless is also acceptable. The "I Am Sufficient" statement leads to "I Am Limitless," for when you are sufficient, there are no limits to your sufficiency. When you look at yourselves, you don't say, "I'm sufficient as long as I wear red pants." There are no limits. There are no red pants. Besides, as a fashion statement, it wouldn't be very good.

CHAPTER FOUR

That Which You Are Is That Which I Am, and That Which I Am Is That Which You Are

The Fourth Defining Statement

To begin, notice that we first said, "That Which You Are Is That Which I Am," rather than, "That Which I Am Is That Which You Are." The first part of the statement is designed to be the first part, the second part is designed to be the second part. Why? Because in truth, most times individuals observe that which others are; they observe around themselves. Most individuals don't begin by observing themselves; they begin by observing outside of themselves. They look at friends, acquaintances and strangers; they look at interactions, relationships, circumstance and situation, and as a result of all of these observations, they begin to discover themselves.

When we suggest to individuals to observe themselves, we suggest to observe without judgment and to observe circumstances, decisions, choices, relationships, and situations–in other words, to observe that which is within and that which is without. Now, we don't suggest doing this in a specific format or direction. We don't say to observe without first and within second, or within first and without second. We suggest simply to observe. Most individuals, when given that suggestion, will begin the process of observation by observing that which is outside of themselves.

Why? Because that is what they perceive on a daily basis. Every day, every aspect of their day, they observe outside of themselves. They observe the car that is cutting them off. They observe the person who is walking across the street. They observe the wife or the husband who is interacting with them. They observe the child who is demanding. They observe the boss who says do this and do that. They observe the car and how it acts. They observe the dog and how it's responding today. They observe everything, but they don't observe themselves. They don't observe their thoughts and their feelings–at least, not at the beginning.

And as a result, they begin a process of observation that is directed toward that which is not of themselves. Therefore, when you define your existence from the perspective of interaction, of interconnection between one and another and all, the statement that we've suggested begins to define that particular interconnection from the perspective that is outside of the self.

Notice that this statement describes an interconnection between that which is outside of the self and that which is within the self. The statement is, "That Which You Are, Is That Which I Am"–and we're just looking at the beginning of this particular statement. For the statement in its totality is in two parts; the first part is what we're examining at this point.

From the perspective of the first part, let's break it down. What is "that which you are"? Begin the process of observation from that perspective. Pick what you wish to pick. Is it the wife, the son, the daughter, the husband, the grandmother, the great-grandmother, the grandfather? Is it the girlfriend, the boyfriend, the guy next door, the cat, the dog, the horse, the cow, the tree, the grass?

Any aspect that you can observe, whether it be through your five physical senses or through an expansion of your sixth sense (your sense of perception), is the "you" in this particular statement. *You* describes anything that is outside of the self. It is not limited. Remember the third statement of our particular statements of existence? It is that you are limitless. Therefore, why limit the perception of *you* in this particular statement? Why say that *you* is only this person, that person, this thing or that thing? Why limit the *you?*

We would suggest instead, give yourselves the broad perspective of unlimitedness so that when you define the *you*, you define it as something and everything outside of the self. *You* becomes everything. It becomes the air you breathe, the sky you perceive, the stars you see at night, the Moon, the Sun, the planet. It becomes everything that forms an integral part of this particular planet. It becomes all life forms, regardless of origin, regardless of circumstance. It becomes the virus, the bacteria. It becomes the person. It becomes the relationships. In other words, as we suggested here, it is everything, anything, and in its totality, from one perspective, it is nothing. It is simply *you*.

Even nothingness can be defined as *you*. It doesn't have to be something. It can be nothing. *You* becomes everything. Therefore, when you perceive it, perceive the *you* in this statement as an expansion of everything that exists; that doesn't exist; that encompasses all of existence, past, present, future, in relation to this existence; that encompasses all existence–whether it be third, fourth, fifth or sixth dimension, or even ourselves from the twenty-ninth, or God/Goddess/The All That Is on the thirty-second dimension of reality. Regardless of the perception of reality, *you* is everything outside of the self.

That's a fairly good opportunity for observation. If you were to begin to observe all of the *you* we're suggesting here, even through your five physical senses, you would not complete this particular observation in your lifetime, we assure you. It would take many hundreds of thousands of lifetimes to observe that which we are suggesting. But at least–and this is key–when you begin to observe, you observe all that exists around you.

Now, the statement says, "That Which You Are." It doesn't say "that that you are," "that could be that you are," "that might be that you are," "that should be that you are." It simply defines "that which you are," not that which you were, not that which you will be. Notice, it's *that which you are.* "That" is a fairly expansive word. It encompasses everything. "Which" defines all aspects of the *you.* "You" defines all aspects of existence. "Are" defines the moment. Think of it in those terms, and then it becomes limitless, expansive, broadening and most of all, creative. For you, dear friends, are creative energy.

As a result, when you begin to observe that which you are, if you apply that statement from within the self, you look outside of the self. Then you observe all of existence.

Now, the next part of this particular section of the statement is, "That Which You Are Is That Which I Am." It's not "might be," "could be," "should be," "ought to be," "well, maybe, you never know," "sometimes, not always." In other words, there are no statements that allow you to wiggle out of this particular concept, this particular perception of consciousness. This isn't something that you apply in one minute and then remove in the next. It defines your existence, regardless of the circumstances of your existence. And we will go into some examples.

However, the key is to recognize that the "Is" is a very powerful statement. The word *Is* is power. It brings power to this statement. Think of it. "That Which You Are Is That Which I Am." "That which" in the second part of this first part of the statement is the same as the first part in the first part of the statement. In other words, "That Which" has the same value.

"I Am": Define the *I.* Is it my personality, my ego? Is it myself? Is it the physical, the mental, the emotional, the spiritual, or all of the above? This is a multiple-choice question here. Is it the consciousness, the subconsciousness or the higher self? Is it the ego-personality or the soul-essence? Is it the soul-essence from a specific dimensional reality, or is it even the extension of the soul-essence from God/Goddess/The All That Is? Is the *I* in this statement limited?

These are questions to ponder. We assure you, however, regardless of which direction you ponder them in, you will uncover for yourselves the limitlessness of this statement. There are no limits to the *I* in the "I Am." There is nothing that stops you, nothing that limits you, nothing that defines you, nothing that gives you boundaries, nothing that creates belief structures. It is simply a statement that describes your existence.

And think of it, what an amazing statement! "That Which You Are Is That Which I Am." View it from this perspective: "That Which You Are Is That Which We Are." We've switched the "I Am" to "We Are" in order to give you this perspective. We, The Wonders, encompass all that you are. We've been asked many times, by many individuals, "Am I part of you?" And often we suggest to individuals, from one perspective, yes. From another perspective, however, you are a direct incarnation of a soul-essence at a certain degree of dimensional reality. But from one perspective, all of those incarnations below the twenty-ninth dimension of reality form part of that which we are. Even the other collective consciousness that exists on our dimensional reality forms part of that which we are. True, we are still separate, and we still perceive a certain degree of separateness; that is what maintains us separate from God/Goddess/The All That Is. But we recognize that that which you or they are is that which we are or I am. We recognize this.

Look around you. Take a look at the person next to you. "That Which You Are Is That Which I Am." Your thoughts, feelings, desires and your choices eventually make up and form part of that which I am. View it from this perspective: Every action, every thought, every inaction that occurs, regardless of circumstance or situation, forms part of that which you are. The fact that you are not consciously aware of it, that you consciously choose not to be involved with it, or to move with it, or to allow yourselves to use that as part of your experience of growth—that is your choice. But regardless of how you choose, "That Which You Are Is That Which I Am" applies.

View it from this perspective: When you say the statement, "That Which You Are Is That Which I Am," you connect. You recognize the interconnection of your existence to another. The same applies to every combination of this group, including every combination that includes this one. "That Which You Are" extends to "That Which I Am"; it forms part of it, encompasses it, moves through it, moves beyond it and as a result, helps to create the reality in which you exist.

Your reality, dear friends–this illusion you call reality, this planet, these trees, this house, the road, the cars, the jobs, the circumstances, the relationships, all of that which you describe as a reality, that which you can sense through your five physical senses–all of that is part of the *you.* And if it is part of the *you*, it is part of the "I Am."

Therefore, when you begin to define your existence and to observe that definition of your existence, you begin to discover through observation the interconnection of the *you* to the "I Am." You observe this interconnection sufficiently to recognize that when you denigrate *you*, you denigrate *I.* When you go to someone and say, "Do you know, you're a fat pig?" we would suggest, take a hard look at who you're denigrating. We assure you, it isn't the person you perceive as a fat pig. Rather it is yourself, for you reduce yourself.

When you go to another and say, "You are doing this; you make me angry; you create my reality; you affect my choices," we assure you that you're not denigrating another, you're denigrating yourself. For in truth, you are saying to yourself, "You is I." And as a result, in every aspect of your existence where denigration of another takes place, you are denigrating yourself.

Now, let's apply this to your present existence, to your society. Let's look at your society. You've created a society that is dependent on mechanization, that is dependent on certain chemical structures. You use pesticides, insecticides, fungicides, regularly. You chlorinate your water, you fluoridate your water, you add poison upon poison into your water, and then say to yourselves, "This is the best water that I can drink."

You take food, you take from the planet, you take from the Earth. You grow food in the same area, drawing all the minerals, all the vitamins, all the substances from the planet Earth, and then you wonder why your food isn't growing. So you spray it with chemicals and chemical fertilizers. Then because it's growing too fast, because the pests are coming after it, you spray pesticides. And why are the pests coming after it? Because there is no life force; it's dead or dying. As a result, pests love it. Yet you still use spray. You spray insecticide so that no insects that will come near it. Why? Because these insects would ravage your crop. Yet you eat this food. You denigrate your body. And then you eat and eat and eat and eat to the point of obesity, and then wonder why your body is reacting the way it is. You denigrate yourselves.

You get into relationships. You are born of parents, and you are parents; as a result of this, you extend belief structures from one "parenthood" to another "parenthood." Do you nurture, do you love? Or do you abuse instead? You sexually abuse, you physically abuse, you mentally abuse. But who do you abuse? The child who is innocent, or yourself?

When you hit another, who are you hitting? If you perceive the concept that we're suggesting here, "That Which You Are Is That Which I Am," every time you take up your hand to hit another, you are hitting yourself. Every time you denigrate another, you denigrate yourself. Every time you hurt another, you hurt yourself. Every time you reduce another, you reduce yourself.

When you take from another, you take from yourself. Let's say you go through the grocery store and the clerk hands you back change; in so doing, she hands you an extra dollar. The clerk can't quite count, and even though the computer tells her what to put as change in your hand, she doesn't do it right. When you take it and you walk away, who are you taking from? The clerk? The grocery store, the company that the clerk works for? No, you take from yourself because you are an extension of that company. That company is an extension of you. "That Which You Are

Is That Which I Am." These are fairly simplistic examples, but they are very accurate.

How many individuals have you heard say that it is easy to steal from the insurance companies? "Oh, the insurance companies are large, they don't mind the waste." Or the government-"Why support the government?" "That Which You Are Is That Which I Am." If your government is restrictive, it is because you are restrictive. If your government is unfair, it is because you are unfair. If your government cheats, it's because you cheat. Do you think the politicians you elect are not an example of yourself? Do you think for one minute that these particular politicians who are intent on power and greed are not a reflection of your own self? Their incompetence is an absolute reflection of your own incompetence, we assure you. Why? Because you chose them. You placed them there. You make choices that reflect back to you "That Which You Are Is That Which I Am."

Think of it. Every choice you make fits the parameters of this particular statement, every choice. Not half, not a quarter, not a third, not even seventy or eighty percent–one hundred percent of every choice that you make. All choices count, not even one escapes. There is not even an opportunity for one little choice to walk away and not be part of this statement. Every choice reflects this statement, "That Which You Are Is That Which I Am."

Very hard, isn't it, to walk away from this? "How is

it possible that the guy down the street, who goes out and shoots his wife and two kids, is a part of me? How is that possible?" That is a good statement, a good question. It is possible because you have created a society and because you form a part of the society that has created the circumstance that allows this individual to be in that particular circumstance and therefore make that choice. Now, we're not suggesting here to stop him. Far from it. But we are suggesting you be aware that "That Which You Are Is That Which I Am."

Now, let's explore the next part of this statement. The next part is the reverse. And we need to explore this now in part, in order to expand on the concepts we are talking about. "That Which I Am Is That Which You Are"–what an interesting statement! Now from within, you go without. Now from inside the self, you go to the outside.

Let's take the example of this person who goes out and shoots his wife and two children. "That Which You Are Is That Which I Am"; therefore, if he is crazy, or depressed, or denied, or denigrated, then so are you. Therefore, the next part of the statement is "That Which I Am Is That Which You Are." The choices you have made have extended into his existence to create a circumstance that allows him to make that choice.

You are creator. There is no need for us to go into a discussion of the "I Am" in "That Which I Am" or the "You Are" in "That Which You Are." We've already discussed this. But what we can provide for you is the benefit of this perspective: From an inside perspective, when you view yourself as "That Which I Am" and you extend it outward to recognize that "that" is "That Which You Are," observe how easy it is to recognize how much of yourself you project outward.

As you walk down the street, someone looks at you with a glance askew. You take it that he doesn't like your dress, and you get offended. What are you observing? Are you observing his dislike? Or are you observing your dislike, your insecurity, your desire to reduce yourself? We assure you, you are observing yours. You've projected that which is within the self to that which is without the self.

That individual could very well have been looking at you and admiring the dress. He sees a good-looking, sexy young woman and says to himself, "That woman is absolutely amazing." Yet from your perception, you criticize yourself. You reduce yourself. You say to yourself, "That person doesn't like my dress. What's wrong with my dress? Is it too short? Is it too long? Is it too tight? Is the cleavage too low, too high? The arms are not covered. Should they be covered? Is the back not right? Is it not wrong? Is it dirty? It doesn't sit right, doesn't fit right, doesn't look right."

And you come up with a million reasons to denigrate yourself. And so you begin to denigrate that person. You put him down; you make him "less than"; you blame him; you accuse him; you make him wrong. When you make another wrong, you are projecting from within yourself. It is your perception of yourself that you are imposing on another. You bring about to yourself this imposition that "that which you are is not sufficient."

Notice this statement, "that which you are is not sufficient." Do you see how it all works? From the first, "Existence Is But an Extension of Yourself"; the second, "I Am Sufficient"; the third, "I Am Limitless; My Choices Reflect My Limitlessness"; to the fourth, "That Which You Are Is That Which I Am, and That Which I Am Is That Which You Are." Notice the connection, the interconnection of all of these statements. You cannot possibly look at the fourth without looking at the first, the second and the third. You can look at the first on its own. You can look at the second on its own. You can look at the third on its own. And you can look at the fourth statement on its own. But then you limit that exploration, and you create an insufficiency in your limitedness. Then you do not discover the interconnection of yourself to another and the interconnection of another to yourself. And as a result, you don't define your existence because you don't see how existence is an extension of everything that you are.

All of these statements speak of the same truth. In a different fashion, true, but the same truth. And the truth is, you are God/Goddess/The All That Is, and you are "That Which You Are."

Think of it. When you see yourself as "That Which I Am," how much of yourself have you begun to observe? When you begin to observe the "I Am," you begin to observe your psychology, your belief structures, your perceptions of yourself. When you observe the "You Are," you observe the physicality, the extension of "That Which I Am." You observe the physicality of that which surrounds you, and to a degree, you observe the emotional connection of that which surrounds you. But you do not truly begin to observe belief structures, limitations and perceptions until you recognize that those reside in the "I Am." Everything around you is a perception created within the "I Am."

Think of it. Four people are standing on a street corner, and along comes a man on a bicycle, carrying a gun. This man stops, goes into the corner store, brandishes his weapon, robs the patron, gets back on his bike, and off he goes. The four individuals are then asked to give a description of what occurred.

The first, feeling that he is a very astute observer, observes that the bicycle rider was actually about five foot six, wearing black shorts and sunglasses and was stooped over his bicycle. He did not see him go into the store and did not see him go out.

The second, also an astute observer, observed that this individual came rushing up, jumped off his bike, went into the store, came running out in a hurry, and left in a hurry with a look of shear panic on his face. He can't describe the face. It looked nondescript, perhaps white skin. But he was wearing a yellow helmet. "That much I noticed," he says.

The third, a female, when asked for her observations, says, "I was too frightened, but I did notice this. The individual was actually five foot nine, weighed about a 152 pounds, had long black hair, a fairly muscular chest and really good-looking legs." "Did you notice anything else?" she was asked. And this person says, "Oh yes, he had a backpack on his back."

The fourth, also female, when asked for her observations–and this is a very astute observer–says, "Right, it was a ten-speed bike, green in color, with the lettering 'mountain bike' on it. And the individual had gloves on his hands, was about five foot nine, weighed about a 170 pounds, had multicolored racing glasses, a yellow and black helmet, a purple vest with black on the back, a backpack over one shoulder, and he was wearing racing pants, racing shorts, no socks and racing shoes. I did not see this person go into the store, but I did see him stop, and then I saw him get back on his bike and leave."

Each one had a different observation, a different perspective of the events that occurred. And what was the truth? The truth encompassed all of it. It wasn't one perspective over another. No one person was completely observant of everything that occurred. They observed that which resonated with them at that moment. Each one, believing that they were very observant, observed what they perceived was everything. And yet, they only observed a portion of the observation. They projected outward "That Which I

Am Is That Which You Are," that my observation is only an observation of "That Which I Am." Thus each one was different.

When they finally caught this individual, he was actually six foot two, 240 pounds, with a black and yellow helmet, a purple, yellow and red shirt and no backpack, but he did have a gun and was riding an 18-speed bike with crazy lettering on it. Some were close, some were partly close. Each observed a portion, none the totality. What they also didn't observe was that this individual was very frightened, very fearful, very unsure. They didn't observe their feelings, they didn't observe how they felt about it–they didn't observe how fearful and scared they were. Had they observed that, they would have observed it within the man.

As a result, they only had partial observations, though from one perspective, very accurate ones. Apply the statement, "That Which You Are Is That Which I Am, and That Which I Am Is That Which You Are," to this observation. Each individual expressed a perspective that was based on an extension of themselves. The one who observed the good legs and the strong muscles–that was important to that individual. Why? Because that individual, at that point in time, was on the lookout for a good mate. The fourth observer, who had a fairly complex description of the individual–one that was accurate to a certain degree–what was she observing? She was observing the portion of herself that was observant. In other words, she was a very observant person, had trained herself to observe to a great degree, and she was beginning to observe herself. As a result, she went deeper into the observation than the others. And yet, not deep enough. She did not observe the state of mind, the state of emotion that the individual was in, or that she herself was in.

Each one observed differently, but each only observed that which would be defined as the "I Am." Now, why did we go to great lengths to describe this little example for you? View it from this perspective: When you walk down the street and you look at something and you observe that something, you are observing a part of yourself, regardless of what that something is. It could be a fruit in a window of a fruit market, or it could be the person chewing on the fruit. It could be the sensuous way the lips wrap themselves around the fruit, or it could simply be the fact that a fly is running around the head of the person eating the fruit. It could be anything. But whatever your observation is, you are observing a portion of yourself.

Which part of you would you like to observe? Which part of you are you looking to expand at that moment? Which part of you are you not observant of? For if you perceive that which you observe, you can also be aware of that which you do not observe. True, to a degree, it would be difficult to observe that which you do not observe, for you wouldn't have observed it. But we assure you that, eventually, you would observe that which you have not observed previously. Which part of yourself are you denying?

For example, if you did not observe the sensual, sexual, succulent way that the woman was chewing into that peach, are you not denying your sensuousness, your sexuality, the succulence of yourself? If all you observe is a fruit sitting in the window, are you not observing your practicality to a degree, your limited perception? Did you observe that this fruit is ripe and succulent? Did you observe the deliciousness of it? No, you simply observed that there was a fruit in the window. Does that not define how you observe your existence? In other words, you go through your existence observing only that which you perceive you need to observe and don't move beyond the practical, logical, spartan perspective–"Let us not look at the creative perspective." What about the color of the skin of the peach, how it melds the yellows, the oranges, the reds and sometimes the greens? Did you observe that?

An artist observes from an artist's perspective; a dentist observes from a dentist's perspective; an accountant from an accountant's perspective; a lawyer from a lawyer's perspective; a judge from a judge's perspective; a housewife from a housewife's perspective. Why? Because each one perceives himself/herself as being a lawyer, a dentist, an accountant, an artist, a housewife. They don't see themselves beyond that. What if the accountant saw himself as an artist, or the lawyer as a housewife, or the doctor as a judge–or any other combination? Expand the self, then the perceptions expand.

Therefore, when you observe "That Which You Are," recognize how limited that observation is. For in the limitedness of your observation, you will recognize your limitedness of "That Which I Am." And when you observe yourselves—for sometimes individuals become intent in self-observation, in self-growth, and you fail to observe everything else that exists around you, and you fail to observe your interconnection to all that exists around you—observe the limitedness of your observation.

True, observing the self has a certain degree of benefit, but it is no greater and no less than the degree of benefit of observing the "You Are." They must be coupled; they must be joined. Notice that our statement did not say, "Do one; don't do the other." We didn't say, "That Which You Are Is That Which I Am," and leave it there. We didn't stop; we didn't end the statement; we didn't leave it that the observation of you is sufficient to observe the "I Am." We didn't limit it. Why? Because we didn't want to give you a limited perspective of existence. For existence is an interconnection, a flow back and forth of all that exists within it. Therefore, it isn't just "That Which You Are Is That Which I Am." It is also "That Which I Am Is That Which You Are."

Take a look around you. Take a look at your society, your existence, your planet. Some of you are content to put great heaps of garbage in certain areas of your planet. You bury it in the hopes that eventually it will turn to oil. We assure you, it will take a few million years to do so. In the meantime, a great deal of usable resources have been disposed of.

Think of it. Your garbage dumps on your planet are like zits on your face. Not much difference. The zit on your face is a toxin that is releasing itself from within. The garbage dumps on your planets are toxins that you have created as a society and are attempting to bury. But they are resurfacing, going to the surface, regardless. The Love Canal dump is a perfect example of that. Remember that not too long ago, all of a sudden, all of this toxic waste rose to the surface. Take a look at your dumps around you. Just in this area alone [Toronto, Canada], you have a dump that is leaching toxic waste, and now you're looking to find ways of stopping that. In fact, you create a space to dump garbage, knowing that the garbage will turn into toxic waste, and then you hope to control it. You hope to destroy it or at least control it sufficiently so that when it leaches into the environment, it will not affect you, the residents surrounding it; or at least, you won't be living next to the dump.

Ever ask a dump manager where he lives? We assure you, it's not right next door to the dump. Ever ask a politician where his or her house is? We assure you, it's not right next door to the dump. There isn't one politician living on top of a dump. Interesting, isn't it? But every politician in your society creates these dumps. Why? Because you give them the power to do so. Why? Because you choose not to make a decision that would remove the ability to create garbage from your society. There are methodologies and techniques that would stop this. But it would require a different perspective, an alternate desire. Do you think for one moment that the technology to eliminate non-biodegradable waste does not exist? We assure you, it exists. It's just not financially feasible to bring it about yet. "Let's create bigger dumps, bigger crises, and when it becomes totally financially viable, then we will put this technology to good use." That's the psychology that exists in your society; that's the psychology that exists within yourselves.

Take a look at your existence. How many of your issues, how many of your belief structures are you looking at? You don't look at them unless they create a crisis in your existence. For example, two individuals are in a relationship, in a marriage, both interacting. After twelve years of interaction, however, they find themselves frustrated and angry to the point that they finally say, "Enough. I'm going my way, you go yours." But neither one of them is willing to examine why they came to that point, long before they got to that point. Once one person leaves, the other says, "Oh, dear God. Why am I being abandoned, why am I alone? It's time to look at myself." And the other says, "Why did I create this? It's time to look at myself." And off you go looking at yourselves. You observe yourselves, you examine yourselves, and you gain a certain degree of self-confidence and another level of security. Then you go into another relationship, hoping beyond hope that this relationship won't end the same way the previous one did.

But you have yet to examine why this was created. Why was it created? Because nobody in the relationship was willing to say, "These are my feelings, these are my thoughts. Can we expand on them, can we share them, can we at least observe them? It is my responsibility to ensure that my feelings are adequately examined and taken care of." No one is willing to take responsibility for themselves or the choices they are making in that relationship. As a result, they don't. Isn't that what your society is all about? Isn't that what your politicians are all about? Isn't that what the choices you're making are all about?

Think about it. You elect someone to do your dirty work. You want more money, so you elect someone who will cut your taxes. But when they cut the taxes and they borrow, and you find out that you have to pay interest on that, then you go and elect someone who's going to raise the taxes so that you can pay off the interest and then hopefully get back into a different economic circumstance.

But then when they do, you get angry at them. And then you don't elect them the next time because they hurt you. "Please tax the other fellow. Don't tax me. Take his money, not mine. I don't have enough to give.

But I want to borrow. I want everything that I want without having to pay for it, and I want you, the government, to give it to me. And then when I have to pay for it, I don't want you to take it from me. I want you to take it from my next-door neighbor. He's got more than I've got. After all, he has the bigger pool in his back yard. Mine's only sixteen feet and his is eighteen feet. He's got more money than I've got."

This is the psychology you live with. This is the psychology that permeates your society. Now, we're not saying this is true of each of you. But we are saying, take a look around you and take a look at yourselves. We assure you, there are belief structures within yourselves that exist in your society, that are manifest in your society. "That Which I Am Is That Which You Are." Observe yourselves, and you'll observe your society. Observe your society, you'll observe yourselves. Do you see how it goes?

Observe the world. Take a look at the world. There is fighting in Yugoslavia. There is fighting in the Middle East. There is fighting in Pakistan and India. There is fighting in China and Taiwan. There is fighting in Russia. There is fighting in South America. There is fighting in Central America. There's even fighting between Canada and the United States. True, the fighting between Canada and the United States is rather mild. We don't go to war. We don't send men off to kill each other. What we do is threaten them instead. "We are going to go home and take our toys with us.

We don't like what you're doing." The Americans are very good at this. "We want you to do what we want you to do, and if you don't want to do what we want you to do, we'll take our money and go home. And if you don't do what we want you to do, we're going to complain to our parent." And who's the parent? It's the world organization that oversees everything. That's the parent. But who controls the parent?

The macrocosm of your existence is the microcosm of all of existence. The microcosm of your existence is the macrocosm of all existence. It goes back and forth. "That Which You Are Is That Which I Am, and That Which I Am Is That Which You Are."

Do you think for one moment that you're enlightened beings? If you do, may we suggest that you observe all that exists around you. Enlightenment is not the wisdom of others, it is the wisdom of the self. Society is not yet enlightened. True, there are a few beings who have a certain degree and proficiency of enlightenment, but they are not enlightened beings. They are partially enlightened. In other words, they're enlightened to a certain point. We would not suggest that they are enlightened beings. They are moving toward enlightenment, yes. So is your society. As quickly as you are willing to change yourselves, so too is your society willing to change itself.

Think of it. How many of you are willing to change and shift and alter your choices in the moment? Not many. Most of you spend years justifying to yourselves why you should do this and why you should do that, instead of saying, "I choose to do this, I choose to do that." You spend years. Some of you spend only months and some of you might only spend days, but as a whole it takes years.

Take a look at your government. How long has it been for the government of this particular country you call Canada to make a decision to allow same-sex relationships as a basis for mutual appreciation? Take a look at the United States. How long was it before a black was allowed to ride at the front of the bus? Not that long ago, one individual was dragged behind a truck until he was torn to pieces. True, there was an outcry. It lasted for about thirty seconds, a new spot in the news, and then that was it. What has changed? What has altered? Everybody had their say, everybody said, "Shame! Woe is me!" And some said, "Good for him." But nothing changed.

Why? Because no one was willing to take responsibility for themselves and say, "I am a bigot. Society reflects my bigotry, and as a result, I will change so that society will change." Now, some of you will argue, what can one person do to change all of society? One bigot, one racist becoming an appreciative individual cannot change all of society. We would say, far from it. You cannot appreciate what you are not. How can you appreciate racism unless you have, to a certain degree, observed racism within yourselves? We assure you, everyone reading this particular book is, to some degree, racist.

Think of that statement. How many of you would scrunch a cockroach? But does the cockroach not have the ability to live the same as you? Now, you would say, "That's not racist." And we would suggest, why not? A cockroach is a race. How many of you would view blacks, whites, Pakistanis, Indians, Japanese, Chinese, Russians, Americans–regardless of how you define them–how many of you have choice comments for those particular races?

"Americans are bullheaded and pigheaded." That statement has been made. "Canadians are wusses, no backbone." "French Canadians are a pain in the . . ." "English Canadians, they're even worse than French Canadians." The Irish Catholics are against the Irish Protestant. How many of you would look at an Irish Catholic or an Irish Protestants and say they're wrong? They're not wrong; they just make choices that they themselves cannot perceive as being an extension of themselves. The Catholic does not see that that which he is that which you are, and that which you are is that which he is. He doesn't see that, and neither does the Protestant. As a result, you have wars between the Catholics, the Protestants, the Muslims, the Christians, the blacks, the whites, the reds, the yellows, the greens, the oranges. Greens and oranges–yes, we assure you, wars are existing in this universe far beyond this planet, and greens and oranges do exist.

Take a look at your metaphysics. Just take a look.

"The archangels are fighting the forces of evil, the angels are protecting all of existence. There are black forces at work, dark forces at work. Entities are taking me over. Entities have caused me to do this, entities have caused me to do that. I am the way I am because of archangels, the angels, these entities, those entities." We assure you, all of this is simply an extension of the unwillingness to perceive that "That Which You Are Is That Which I Am, and That Which I Am Is That Which You Are."

When the archangel is fighting the forces of evil, who's fighting it? Not the archangel, we assure you. That is only a perception. It is a perception that is projected onto a realm that goes beyond the physical into the metaphysical in such a way that your existence can be abdicated. Your responsibility for your existence can be abdicated. "It's not my fault, it's the archangel's fault; he didn't do his job, he didn't protect me. After all, if Jesus Christ hadn't been a wuss and died on the cross, we wouldn't have these problems, would we?"

These are thoughts, we assure you. We're not suggesting these words ourselves. They are thoughts that have existed in other peoples' minds. And they use these as excuses to abdicate their own responsibility to their existence. "It's your fault, not mine." "You created this, not me." "It's the politician who caused this problem, not me." "It's the guy next door who didn't want to give his pool away, and because he didn't, I had to pay taxes. It's his fault, not mine."

"We have garbage dumps. That's not my fault. I only produce 6.2 tons of garbage a year. It's the other people who produce the other 150 tons a year. Mine was a measly 6.2. It's not my fault." "It's not my fault that the person next door shot his wife and children. It's not my fault. True, I noticed that he wasn't quite together. I noticed that he was depressed. And I noticed that he needed someone to talk to, but I didn't have the time. It's not my fault."

Every aspect of your existence is an extension of yourself. "That Which You Are Is That Which I Am, and That Which I Am Is That Which You Are." Fascinating. And we are you as much as you are we, which is why we choose to interact with you at this time in your existence. Because we are attempting to heal ourselves, we are attempting to expand and extend ourselves. And we love ourselves, which is why we love you.

Additional Comments

On the notion that Gaia and animals have a consciousness that is separate from our own

From one perspective, each one has a separate consciousness to a degree, and therefore you perceive them as separate from the self. You perceive the animal, the tree, the planet, as being separate from the self. As a result, in your projection of your own particular energy, you project a certain degree of perception of separateness into another. Therefore, there is in your perception a consciousness that is "not of your own consciousness," and so you perceive it as being separate.

The dove standing by your side has a separate consciousness, a separate free will, a separate free choice. To a degree, that is correct. It is correct from your perspective as an ego-personality of being separate from all of existence. But what we are suggesting is that even you as ego-personality are an extension of soul consciousness, and therefore, from that perspective, that dove beside you is also an extension of soul consciousness.

We know that as ego-personalities, you would like to believe that you have a particular soul consciousness that is separate from this soul consciousness, that is separate from that soul consciousness, that is separate from this other's soul consciousness, that is separate from that other's soul consciousness. But we would suggest, dear friends, that the need to perceive separateness comes from the perspective of the ego, not from the perspective of soul-essence.

True, we provided you with a perspective of dimensional reality existence: There are soul consciousnesses that exist on the ninth dimension of reality, the tenth, the twelfth, and we exist on the twenty-ninth, and God/Goddess/The All That Is exists on the thirty-second. But at no time did we say they were separate. We simply said that they exist on a different dimension of reality. That a soul-essence does exist, true. The dimension of reality is a perspective of a perspective of existence, but it does not define separateness. Now, we recognize that by giving you a model that is based on thirty-second dimensions of reality, it satisfies the ego-personality's need for linearity, for separateness, for "greater than" and "lesser than" perspectives. But that was not the intent when we gave it. When we gave it, we gave it as a perspective that would provide individuals with an opportunity to recognize that "That Which They Are Is That Which We Are." And as a result, by observing ourselves, they can observe themselves.

Therefore, to a degree, the perspective of the separateness of the dog, the cat, the horse, the cockroach, the tree, the branch, Gaia—all of these simply come from a perspective that is centered in the ego-personality's need to define itself as separate from all of existence. How can an ego-personality define itself as separate if it does not separate everything from itself? It is not a question of ego-personality being separate from all of existence. It is that each and every aspect of it must be separate in order for it to accept its own separateness. For if it was the world against you, we assure you, it wouldn't take long for you to join the world.

Therefore, the necessity to perceive this separateness resides with the ego and ego-personality. Soul-essence, as it moves and progresses, does not perceive itself as separate. True, there is a certain degree of dimensional existence whereby separateness of soul-essence does exist. At least, the perspective exists. It isn't that they are separate; it is that the perspective exists. As we've suggested, up until the thirteenth dimension of reality, there is a certain perspective of separateness of soul-essence from all of existence. Then it moves to a perception of group consciousness, eventually moving to a perception of collective consciousness. But it is only a perception, dear friends. It isn't reality. It isn't about that which exists. It is simply a perception. Even ourselves–we recognize that it is our perception that is limiting our experience from God/Goddess/The All That Is. That's all, just a perception. And it is the perception that we are attempting to move through, through our own particular methodologies, through our own expansion of self, in such a way that the perception no longer exists.

Now, for yourselves, we're suggesting that you begin to recognize that the degree of separateness that exists in consciousness can be shifted and altered in such a way that you begin to recognize the interconnectivity of yourselves with all of existence. We're not suggesting yet that you set aside your perception of separateness. That would be too far a leap in consciousness at this point. But what we are suggesting is that you are interconnected, and in that interconnection, you can begin to perceive the illusion of separateness.

Gaia is not separate from your consciousness. The horse, the dog and the cat are not separate from your consciousness. All soul consciousnesses have formed this illusion that you call third-dimensional reality. It is part of an extension of their soul consciousness. Yet that is not separate from their soul consciousness. We ourselves, our energy is extended to form part of this third-dimensional reality, this illusion you call third-dimensional reality. Our energy is extended here. And why wouldn't we be? We are and form part of All That Is, as are you. The difference is, we don't perceive that separateness.

Therefore, when you ask a question of ourselves, we can simply look within ourselves. For we form you just as you form us. The same applies to anyone else. There is no separateness between the dog, the cat and you. But you see it that way because, with your five senses, you see an animal that resides outside of the self. Far be it for us to shatter your illusions, dear friends. It isn't our intent. We are not here to shatter your illusions; we are here to provide you with an opportunity to choose how you perceive your illusions. Then, in the choice of perception, you can expand your illusions. Notice we said "expand your illusions," not "contract." The idea is not to eliminate illusions, the idea is to expand your illusions to the point of recognizing that an illusion is an illusion. And therefore, you can choose to play or you can choose not to play. But it is still an illusion.

View it from this perspective: Presently, you are looking at an individual [René channeling The Wonders] lying in a chair, fairly comfortably we might add, with hands moving up and down playing ticktack-toe on his legs. It's almost like he's playing a flute, maybe a saxophone, perhaps a keyboard. Is that not an illusion? It looks real, it feels real; you hear words, but even that is an illusion. It's an illusion that you're willing to accept. It isn't separate from you; it is an extension of you. However, because your ego-personality perceives itself as a separate existence, it cannot perceive itself as a separate existence unless it perceives all that exists around it as a series of separate existences. It cannot. It would not, cannot justify its own perception unless it perceives all others as being the same as itself. As a result, you are willing to observe this and say this is a separate existence. And we ourselves, from one perspective, agree. Because if we were to tell you and present to you the oneness and wholeness of all that we are in relation to that which you are, you could not accept it. It wouldn't fit your parameters of experience. It wouldn't. You wouldn't be able to observe it, to appreciate it, to encompass it in your existence. Nor would you choose to. There is too much fear.

How many times have we extended ourselves, energy-wise, to provide healing to you? Many times, have we not? And how do we do that? Think of it. It is energy. We are energy, you are energy. We can, if we choose to, increase this energy at this very moment such that you would experience an influx of energy to experience a oneness with all of existence. But if we were to do that, dear friends, we would not honor your choice to perceive yourselves as separate entities. And as a result, we choose not to. And you can sit there, and yes, we know you would wish to say, "But I do want it." We assure you, you don't. Because if you did want it, you wouldn't need us to do it.

You are separate from your perceptions, and as a result, everything around you must be separate within itself. It's like the guy who gets the mailbag. It's a mailbag. There's mail in it. But each envelope within the mailbag is a separate envelope. Yet if he closes the mailbag, all he sees is the bag. True? Open it and he sees all the envelopes. That's a good example, a good analogy of your existence. Close your existence, perceive your existence for what it is, and you'll see that there is no separateness. But you are an envelope among envelopes looking out and saying, "There's a pile of envelopes." And you must do so because you perceive yourself as an envelope, and therefore everything around you must be perceived as separate from you. Otherwise you would not be in control of your existence.

The need to perceive Gaia as a separate consciousness is a need that, in effect, flatters the ego's perspective. The ego needs to see separateness to feed itself. And as the ego-personality expands itself from a perspective of consciousness, it will eventually move to setting aside that need. But until it chooses to, all will be perceived as separate. From one perspective, the statement that we gave you, "That Which You Are Is That Which I Am, and That Which I Am Is That Which

You Are," describes that need, dear friends. Yet observe carefully: It also describes the bag.

As you suggested, "To the extent that you're willing to give up the illusion of seeing yourselves as separate, you would no longer continue to perceive others as separate from yourselves." The defining portion of your statement is "to the extent that you're willing to." As we did suggest, some of you are willing to, to a certain degree, and others will expand to that degree. But we assure you that even the Nazarene perceived himself as separate. That was the experience of this existence. And as we've suggested to you, your spirituality, to a degree, is to experience the experience of this existence. If you were to experience yourselves as a oneness with all of existence, you would not gain an appreciation of your separateness from God/Goddess/The All That Is. You cannot become one with God/Goddess/The All That Is without appreciating the separateness or that which keeps you separate from God/Goddess/The All That. We are presenting to you the perspective that it is simply a perspective that separates you, and until you gain an appreciation of that perspective, you cannot let go of it.

You have to see the separateness, the nonseparateness, and all that is. For you cannot perceive The All That Is until you see separateness and oneness. And both are not separate, one from the other. From a perspective of ego-personality, you perceive separateness as separate from oneness, do you not? "You move to a state of oneness, you let go of a state of separateness. Oneness is different from separateness. It is separate from separateness." We assure you, it is not. Oneness and separateness coexist and become All That Is.

On the perceived benefit of the ego-personality seeing itself as interconnected

The perceived benefit is that by becoming interconnected, it can become greater, more, in the sense that the ego would like to see itself as more. Not "greater than," though, we assure you, the ego is very intent on seeing itself as greater than. Therefore, from that perspective, it has an opportunity to move to that perspective of "greater than." Most ego-personalities move in that direction. But a key benefit to the ego is to perceive itself as greater and in the greater perception, know that its existence is secure.

View it from this perspective: If you had a swimming pool in your back yard that was three feet in diameter, and you were quite content in it, then what would make you move to a swimming pool that was eighteen feet in diameter? Absolutely nothing, unless you could perceive that in the eighteen-foot swimming pool, you would be the same as when you're in the three-foot swimming pool. In other words, it isn't that you would be a large person in a small pool and a small person in a large pool; it is that you would be a large person in a small pool and a large person in a large pool. Once you perceive it from that perspective, the ego would move. In other words, there is no reduction of the self; this is the greater perspective. It expands itself. The ego then perceives itself as expansive in a broader perspective, and as a result, it moves to that perspective.

What ensures the perception of security, from the ego-personality's perspective, is the absence of a big plug in the bottom of the pool. If you pull the plug, there is no pool, we assure you. In other words, that which would ensure that perception to the ego is that it exists in the same relationship to its environment regardless of what the environment is. In other words, the circumstances of existence will not alter and shift to reduce the ego. The ego is fearful of reduction. In fact, we would suggest, why perceive a necessity to reduce? The ego perceives that, by expanding itself, it reduces itself because it expands itself into a greater whole, and therefore, it is a smaller fish in a bigger pond. "Better to be a big fish in a small pond than a small fish in a big pond. As a result, the ego then fights the concept of moving to the big pond." But we're suggesting, if you allow the ego to perceive that it is a big fish in a small pond and a big fish in a big pond, or a bigger fish in a big pond, then it does not fear the shift. For it will perceive itself in terms of equality, as equal in one situation as in the other, in one circumstance as in another. Therefore, show the ego that by expanding itself, it remains the same.

Interesting, isn't it? The more you expand yourselves, the more you remain the same. From the ego's perspective, it doesn't necessarily perceive itself as equal to other energies, but it doesn't fear equality. In the expansion of energy, or in the expansion of consciousness, as you choose to expand your ego's consciousness, you can include, as part of the expansion, the perspective of equality. And then, as a result, it will maintain itself from the perspective of equality, equal to all that exists. And it will not fear that equality, because it would also perceive itself as equal to that which it was. That which is, is that which was. "That Which You Are Is That Which I Am, and That Which I Am Is That Which You Are."

Think of it from the perspective of ego-personality and soul-essence. Think of it from the perspective of what you were yesterday to today. Think of it from the perspective of ego as it grows, moves; shifts consciousness, and perspective. Apply that statement to your question. Do you see the possibilities? Fascinating, isn't it? The ego-personality remains the same, and yet it is not. All is an illusion. Ego-personality needs to maintain the illusion of stability, of sameness, but it is not. And it is not until the one day that the ego-personality realizes it has shifted and changed that it will then allow itself to accept a different paradigm of existence.

On conflicts, such as in Bosnia, being reflective of a conflict within ourselves

If you were to alter and shift yourselves in such a way that, you would heal the conflicts within yourselves–bring about a resolution of conflicts, bring about a movement of energy from all aspects of the self–the war in Bosnia would not necessarily end in the moment that you do. Your particular healing, dear friends, would bring about a shift in mass consciousness in such a way that then mass consciousness can, if it chooses to, also shift its own consciousness on an individual and collective basis to that perspective. And then, provided a sufficient amount of individuals choose to, the mass consciousness will shift sufficiently to allow a healing, a resolution to take place in the Bosnian conflict.

Family conflicts are the same. You are part of the reality. It isn't just simply your creation; it is also the creation of the other members of your family. They have free will and free choice. If you have a conflict within yourself that you extend outward to your family, they then have free will and free choice to extend that to you. Once you resolve your conflict, they may then choose to stop extending that extension of yourself to you, true. But by that time, they might have developed a conflict within themselves to the point that they enjoy the circumstances they find themselves in and would say to themselves, "Why stop?"

They have free choice and free will. We're not suggesting that that would be the answer, but they do have free choice and free will. Once you extend your energy outward and it returns to you as a result of the free choice and free will of others to return it to you, they can also maintain that by choosing to extend it from within themselves. It is not simply a return to you. We assure you, it does not bounce off a wall and come back to you. It comes through other individuals, and as a result, it is extended back to you. It is not a reflection back to you; it is an extension back to you. Do you understand the difference?

View it from this perspective: Have you ever played tennis? When you bounce the ball against the wall, what happens to it? It comes back to you, true? And as a result, no matter how many times you hit it against the wall, it always comes back to you. The same ball comes back to you.

Now, let us assume that the wall doesn't just bounce the ball back to you, it actually takes it within itself and sends it back to you. It returns it to you in a way that you would perceive it as bouncing back to you, but in actual fact, the wall has added its energy to it. Do you see? Now the ball doesn't simply bounce back to you off a hard object that has no impact on it, the ball is actually returned to you because the wall has an impact on it.

Ever notice, for example, that when you bounce the ball against the wall, when it comes back to you, it doesn't come back to you in exactly the same manner as you sent it to the wall. Take a ball and bounce it, throw it or shoot it–however you wont to do it–straight at a wall with a certain degree of force. When it returns to you, it will not have the same force. It will not be in the same manner. The ball won't be as round as what it was when it left you. It may be perceived that way because your perception is limited. But we assure you, if you were to measure it, it wouldn't be quite the same round, circular object. There would be change; there would be alteration. The fuzz on the tennis ball would be scuffed in one spot. There would be less bounce to the ball. The rubber wouldn't be quite as bouncy. It is changed. It is altered. In other words, the wall added something to it. It's perceived as being bounced back, as being returned to you in the same fashion, but it is not.

And that is what you're doing with the energy around you. When you extend your energy outward and others return it to you, and you perceive them reacting to your energy, they aren't simply returning your energy to you; they are returning your energy coupled with their energy to you. And as a result, when you resolve your circumstances, your conflicts, and we would suggest that you alter that perspective of conflicts–as you resolve your circumstances within yourself to bring about a shift of consciousness, then they may choose not to resolve the circumstances that would bring about a shift in their consciousness. Therefore, their behavior might continue.

"That Which You Are Is That Which I Am, and That Which I Am Is That Which You Are." It isn't just one way. Notice that? We didn't say, "That Which I Am Is That Which You Are." We didn't say, "That Which You Are Is That Which I Am." We said both. The extension of your energy combines with another's energy to extend back to you. Recognize that your need for simplicity in this case, is defined by your ego in order to maintain the separateness of your existence. Think of it. If it was as simplistic as you perceived it to be, you really wouldn't have to work on it, would you? And at the same time, you wouldn't have to recognize your interconnection to all of existence.

We assure you, this statement moves you far beyond the limits of your ego-personality. It can, if you choose, move you to infinity, to God/Goddess/The All That Is, to however you wish to describe it. It can move you to limitlessness beyond your perceived imagination, we assure you. And even then, it will move you beyond that. "That Which You Are Is That Which I Am, and That Which I Am Is That Which You Are." Put that into your consciousness, and play with it. Have fun, observe it, look at it. Turn it upside down, sideways, frontward, backward. Take it home, take it to work. Take it to the bus, take it to the beach, take it on your next plane trip. Take it to the bathroom, take it when you read dirty magazines and take it when you read clean magazines. Take it when you have sex, and take it when you don't have sex. Take it everywhere. In other words, make it part of your existence and observe it. We assure you, it's already entered into your consciousness. That you read these words has entered your consciousness; its your choice as to how much energy you would like to apply to this particular statement. You're looking for a methodology and a technique that would limit it. Why limit it? Part of your psychology is that if it is limited, it is workable. And if it is limitless, then nothing is workable.

You could take a lifetime to explore this concept or you could take three seconds and know it all. You could take ten million lifetimes and never know it all. But regardless of how much time you take, won't it be a fun journey? Therefore, why limit the fun? You see, you look at it as something that must be done–you must do this to get that, must increase your consciousness to get to the next level, must do that to get this. Why? This is about eliminating the word "must" from your language. There is no such thing as "must," unless, of course, you smell musty. And that's another subject entirely.

There is no such aspect as "must" unless you choose to make "must" a part of your existence. We're suggesting to you, set aside the word "must" and simply give yourselves permission to enjoy. You will accomplish as much. In fact, you'll accomplish more. When you apply the word "must," you limit the experience. When you set aside the word "must," you unshackle yourselves from your limits, and then the experience becomes broader, more expansive, more loving and limitless. A limitless experience is, from one perspective, very limitless. Look at it this way: If you must learn to fly, you can do so. But if you must learn to fly with wings of steel, you can do that also. We would suggest, why not simply enjoy flying, and then different aspects will take place? Flying can be done in a physical form, such as the illusion of your reality, in a plane, in a glider, in a parachute, in a parasail. It can be done in a number of ways that are flying. But you can also do it in your dreams, in your astral travels, in your meditations—that is also flying. But if you see it as "must do" only in your reality, you'll never explore beyond the limits of your reality.

Set aside "must"—unless, of course, you're a little ripe, in which case "must" is definitely part your existence. We assure you, the words we've spoken apply to a number of you in this particular group this evening. All of you, set aside the word "must"; instead add the word "enjoy," and please, don't couple them together. Eliminate the word "must," and add the word "enjoy." Enjoy the movement.

We assure you, there are many individuals sitting on the throne first thing in the morning who would enjoy your movement. The same movement applies. It's no different. Eliminate the garbage in your life, and you have movement. Interesting, isn't it. And the same thing applies. Whether you sit or stand, it's the same thing.

We're being playful with you. We hope you enjoy our playfulness. But what we're suggesting here, dear friends, is that you give yourselves the opportunity to explore the limits of this statement. Notice, we said the *limits* of this statement. Once you've explored them, you will find that there are no limits. But until you choose to explore the limits, you cannot find that there are no limits. Therefore, why not give yourselves the chance to explore?

Now, you can, if you choose, add the word "must": You must explore. But we would suggest, instead, add the word "enjoy." Enjoy exploring. Some of you will undoubtedly choose to add both: You must enjoy exploring. And we would suggest, if you choose to, please, you have our permission—not that you needed it. But we would suggest, of greater benefit to yourselves is to explore and enjoy the process.

For you will, dear friends, in the discovery of the process, truly gain—and we repeat, gain—such a joy in your exploration that you will wonder at the amazingness of your own talents and abilities. And you—simple, lowly, individual yous, separate yous—could uncover, discover, appreciate your interconnection, your oneness, your separateness, and your all-that-isness that you will discover is your amazingness. You all have the talents, you all have the abilities to help you in this direction, we would suggest. Satisfied? We cannot add more to this.

That which we could add is this: "That Which You Are Is That Which We Are, and That Which We Are Is That Which You Are." To that end, here is our expression of love to you. Thank you for sharing our existence.

CHAPTER FIVE

That Which You Choose, You Do So Out of Joy

The Fifth Defining Statement

In existence, individuals make choices from day to day and from moment to moment. Every moment is an opportunity to choose. And from that perspective, choice is made. View it from that perspective then. Recognize that each choice that you make, you make because you choose to do so.

Now, individuals would often discuss and disagree with that particular statement. They would say, "But I didn't choose to get hit by the car," or such statements as, "I didn't choose to get raped." So as a result, they would view their existences on the basis of incidences in which they find themselves in and would argue that, consciously, they did not choose those particular circumstances for themselves. For had they the opportunity to choose, they certainly wouldn't have chosen those very circumstances that would inflict pain and sorrow on their existence–their perspective being, "Who would choose pain and sorrow? Only a fool would do so." And we would suggest to you, dear friends, that every choice that you make, you made. Every occurrence in your existence is a choice that you made.

The individual who was hit by the car, for example: That individual chose. Whether consciously, subconsciously or unconsciously, that individual made the choice to place himself in that particular circumstance in order to allow himself to participate in the experience that was created. As a result, the choice was made by him. The individual who was raped: We assure you, that individual made the choices to bring herself to a point of circumstance that allowed herself to participate in the experience of rape. Now, those choices were not conscious from the perspective of ego-personality, and as a result, they could be viewed as subconscious and unconscious. But regardless of how you view the choices–whether you view them as conscious, subconscious or unconscious–the fact remains that they did choose.

Now, why would individuals choose to place themselves in a certain set of circumstances that would inflict on them pain, sorrow or even death? Why would they choose this? We would suggest, dear friends, that the reason that particular choice is made is because they view that choice as being a choice that would bring benefit to their existence.

Now, let's discuss this. Certain individuals would say, "What's the benefit to being hit by a car?" or "What's the benefit to being raped?" And from a perspective of existence—ego-personality existence—it can be argued that the benefit is minimal at best. But move beyond the ego-personality perspective. Move to observing all of the existence, move to observing all of existence complete—past, present and future—and see that that particular incident, circumstance or situation forms a thread to the past, the present and the future, and is therefore integral to all of existence.

Once you allow yourselves to perceive the circumstance or situation from the perspective of the totality of existence, you will recognize that the desire, the reason, the choice made to participate in that particular circumstance was made because the benefit to the individual is to allow him/her to grow beyond a certain perspective of existence—a certain parameter, a certain belief structure, a certain limit that existence itself has been chosen and imposed upon by the ego-personality in that particular circumstance.

As a result, from a certain perspective, it is easy to perceive how a circumstance that would create harm to an individual was chosen as a perspective of benefit. And if chosen as a perspective of benefit, then was that perspective of benefit viewed as being detrimental, as being sorrowful and painful? Or was the perspective of benefit viewed as being joyful?

We would suggest to you, dear friends, and we would assure you that the perspective of benefit is always perceived as joyful. Ego-personality itself may judge the perspective and may judge it from the perspective that it is sorrowful and painful–as opposed to joyful and pleasurable–and thus assigns a certain parameter of definition to the experience or circumstance. But we assure you that when we speak of joy, we speak of the joy of love of experience, of love of existence, in effect, of love of God/Goddess/The All That Is through soul experience, through to ego-personality experience.

As a result, the joy that the choice has been made, in effect, permeates the choice. The joy is a joy that expands the existence. Therefore, from the perspective of expansion, rape or being struck by a car, as in our previous examples, can both have a perspective of joy to the totality of existence. How an individual perceives the experience, from the ego-personality's perspective, determines the reaction to the experience.

But we assure you, regardless of how it is perceived, the choice made to participate in that experience was made from the perspective of joy, from the perspective of expansion of existence. If joy is equated with the expansion of your existence–and we suggest that it is–then the experience is an expansion of your existence. How you perceive it, how you react to it, how you respond to it is a choice you make, and even that choice is also an expansion of your existence.

View it from this perspective: As the result of rape, an individual might find herself fearful, becoming phobic in her fear, and refuse to go out, refuse to involve herself in relationships—refuse to expand her existence, from one perspective. As a result, it is viewed by others that that particular experience was a contracting experience, not an expanding experience. If that individual's judgment had been that it was an expanding experience, things would have moved differently. The individual chose, instead, to contract.

We would suggest that the choice made by that individual to contract her existence is, from one perspective, an expansive choice. It allows her to perceive the benefit of a contracting choice, therefore bringing her to a perspective that would eventually, through circumstance, through choice, through alteration of existence, move her to expand her existence—existence here being defined as the totality of all existence, past, present and future. As a result, she is not limited in that choice.

Recognize what we're saying here. The choices you make, you do so out of joy. You do so because you want to choose. You do so because it brings joy to your existence.

Now, has anyone here heard the phrase that the most negative person loves to be negative? We assure you, many have. Listen carefully to an individual who constantly complains. Those around him usually say, "That one likes to complain so much, he must love to complain." And so he does love to complain.

Why? Because it brings joy to his existence. He chooses to complain, and therefore, that choice is made out of joy. If he didn't want that choice, if that choice brought to him sorrow and pain (lack of joy would be a greater definition), if that choice brought him lack of joy, then that choice would not be made, we assure you. He would not complain. Why? Because it wouldn't be joyful to him anymore. We assure you, a complainer loves to complain because he has fun doing it. It is his greatest pleasure, his greatest joy. He likes to perceive the reactions of others, and he likes the attention that it gives him. As a result, the more he complains, the better he feels. There are also individuals who, the more they hurt themselves, the better they feel. Individuals who, the more they don't love themselves, the better they feel.

It could be argued that *the individuals in our previous example*, who allowed themselves to participate in a circumstance of rape, didn't want that, that they certainly didn't enjoy the action. But we would suggest that what they enjoyed was the awareness that they themselves were "less than." And they allowed themselves to be in a circumstance that reflected this to them.

The extent of the circumstance, the extent of the impact on their existence of that circumstance, can be viewed as the extent to which they themselves are joyful in their existence. The greater the impact, the greater the joy.

Now, from your perspective, dear friends, you judge the impact. You judge on the basis of right and wrong. "This impact is right, this impact is wrong. This impact is good, this impact is bad." And so as a result, you separate your existence. There is the right on the right side and the wrong on the left side, so everything is separated. And if you were to view choice as simply being choice, you would see that there is no left and no right; no right, no wrong; no good, no bad. There is simply choice.

And therefore, the joy of choosing exists, regardless of the result of the choice. It isn't the result of the choice that brings joy to your existence, it is the fact that you choose that brings joy to your existence. The fact that you can choose–that you do choose–is what drives you as ego-personalities, as entities, in this and other existences. It drives you to choose. Why? Because choice is a manifestation of yourselves as extensions of God/Goddess/The All That Is. That is the freedom you have. That is the absoluteness of your existence–that you can choose. That is to your credit. And that, dear friends, is your joy of existence.

Choice reflects your joy, regardless of the outcome of the choice–and this is important to recognize. It isn't the outcome of the choice, it isn't the manifestation of the choice that decides joy. The manifestation of the choice will decide pleasure, it will decide sorrow and pain, but it will not decide joy. Joy comes from the simple act of choosing.

Therefore, we would suggest to you that on the basis that joy is a manifestation or a result of choice, why not give yourselves the freedom to choose whenever you choose to choose. Give yourselves the permission to choose. When you choose to limit your choices, you choose to limit your joy.

Now, we're not suggesting here for even one instant that you go out and make choices upon choices upon choices, regardless of the outcome. For that, dear friends, would mean that you would reexperience all the experiences of your previous existences—and for what purpose? Throughout your existences you've gained an appreciation that certain choices lead you in certain directions, that certain choices have a resultant action, have a resultant circumstance from that choice, and that that resulting circumstance has limited benefit to your existence.

Therefore, why repeat that particular awareness? The awareness already exists. We would suggest that you simply give yourselves permission to choose to expand the limits of your existence in such a way that you recognize the value and validity of choices to your existence and the results of the choices to your existence.

For example, if the individual being raped had been conscious of her particular choices—or had he been conscious of his particular choices—she would have recognized that that particular choice would have led directly to an action which would, in effect, have a certain result in her existence. As a result, that choice would not necessarily have been made the same way.

Would that have limited the existence? No, because that experience has already been experienced through previous choices and previous existences. But what would have occurred is an expansion of the existence, and that, dear friends, is an expansion of love, an expansion of self-love.

When you choose to your benefit, you choose to your self-love. Therefore, you choose to expand the joy in your existence through the expansion of your self-love. In the previous statements, we've suggested to you that you are limitless and that the choices you make reflect your limitlessness. In this statement, we say that you make the choices you make out of joy. Therefore, see the correlation, dear friends: Your limitlessness is an expansion of your joyfulness. The more you limit your existence, the less joy in your existence. The more joy in your existence, the fewer limits in your existence.

Now, do not view limits as, or confuse them with boundaries. Far from it. Boundaries are not limits. To a degree, boundaries are perceived as limits, but they are simply a definition of the self that can be moved at will. The limit we speak of is a limit that, in effect, reduces the self. A boundary, to a degree, is a limit, but not from the perspective of "limitedness" of the self.

Therefore, in your existence, some of you will choose to establish certain boundaries that define your existence. These boundaries become limits when you are so attached to them that you refuse to alter them depending on the circumstance of your existence at that moment. If you choose to move the boundaries as the circumstance of your existence dictates, then you find yourselves limitless. But if you choose to maintain the boundaries, regardless of the circumstance of your existence, then you have established a limit in your existence. Do you see how that works?

The statement, "I Am Sufficient," supports the perspective that the choices you make, you do so out of joy. For in truth, you are sufficient enough to make any choice, regardless of the choice–and therefore joy would permeate your existence. Each statement that we've given you, from the first to now, are intertwined, one to the other. They extend each other; they expand on each other.

Let us review for a moment. "Existence Is But an Extension of Yourself." That was a good statement. It provided you with a certain perspective of what existence is all about. You could look around you and see that certain actions, certain interactions, certain circumstances were truly an extension of yourself, an extension of that which you created. But that which you created, you did so from choice. And "That Which You Choose, You Do So Out of Joy." Therefore, existence is but an extension of your joy. Apply joy in your existence, and the existence becomes limitless. And not only is it limitless, but beyond all of that, it is also sufficient. Interesting how it all works together, isn't it?

Take the second statement, "I Am Sufficient." It expanded on the first. It said quite simply that not only is existence an extension of yourself, but it specifically said, "I Am Sufficient." Not you, not them, not the other guy, not the girl down the street. Not the minister, the priest, the doctor, the lawyer, the politician. It said, "I Am Sufficient"–personal. Why? Because if we had said, "You Are Sufficient," dear friends, you would have taken it as a directive from ourselves. And the statement is not a directive from ourselves.

The first statement, "Existence Is But an Extension of Yourself," is also not a directive from ourselves. We could have said, "of the self," "of itself," "of that self," "of the guy next door." We could have said, "of myself." But if we had said, "Existence Is But an Extension of Myself," then the impact would have been different. We assure you, the word "yourself" was the strongest word possible. For it allowed you to explore yourselves–the inward and the outward of the self. If we had said "myself," you would have gone inward only. By saying, "Existence Is an Extension of Yourself," you went outward.

The second statement, "I Am Sufficient," brought you inward to recognize that "that which you are is sufficient," regardless of circumstance. And in the sufficiency, you create an existence. In addition to that, in your sufficiency you can recognize your limitlessness, which extends to the next statement.

Notice we said, "I Am Limitless; My Choices Reflect My Limitlessness." We didn't say "you," we didn't apply the *you* in this case, because limitlessness was an inward perspective. First, we gave you an outward perspective, then we brought you inward, and now we're bringing you outward again. Why? Because those are the steps necessary for you to expand your existence. The "I Am Limitless" is saying that whatever you choose, there is no limit to the choice. There is no limit to your existence. Therefore, allow yourselves to move beyond your very choices. Choose to choose beyond your choices.

Which brings you to the next statement, "That Which You Are Is That Which I Am, and That Which I Am Is That Which You Are." Notice how we went back and forth, inward, outward, outward, inward. Notice how the focus shifts from totally inward to the outward first and back inward, and then the inward first and back outward. Why? Because you are able to recognize the relationship of that which exists beyond yourselves and that which exists within yourselves, that both are one and the same. No different. All exists as one.

And therefore, if all exists as one, then each choice you make is part of the whole and affects the whole. And what is the whole? From one perspective, it could be said that the whole is you, but it is also God/Goddess/The All That Is. It's the all-encompassing. It's the all-complete. Therefore, if that which is you is also that which is them, and that which is them is that which is you (notice we didn't use those terms, that would have been very confusing; we used the *you* and the *I*), then, dear friends, you are able to recognize the flow of energy as it moves inward and outward and back inward again: or outward and inward and back outward again. Regardless of direction, you choose to begin.

And now the fifth statement, that choice is joy. It comes from joy, it comes from a love of the self. It comes from the perspective of love of the self. Expand the perspective of the self, and you expand the choices. Many times, individuals have approached us and said, "What do I do in these circumstances? I can either go this way or that way. Are these all the choices I have?" And we have and constantly will suggest to these individuals that in truth, by recognizing their own love of self, they are able to expand their perspective of choice. We often give them suggestions for different choices, but regardless of what we do, we always suggest to them, "Go inside and love yourself." We add that, we plant that seed, we discuss that with individuals. We attempt to provide them with the perspective that by loving themselves, they give themselves the permission to expand their joy in their existence.

And as a result of the expanded joy in their existence, choices will also expand in their existence. No longer will they limit themselves to this or that; to left or right; to right or wrong; to good or bad. They will, in fact, expand themselves beyond those aspects, those polarities, to discover that they have multiple opportunities, multiple choices, and that by simply viewing themselves in a loving fashion, they open themselves and their perceptions to observe the joy in their existence. As a result, they expand their perception of choice, which expands the joy.

Notice how every statement is interrelated? There is a sixth statement that we will give you at a later time, and we assure you, this will encompass all of the five. But the key to recognize at this moment is that every choice you make, you do so from a joy of self. Having said that–and we've spent a great deal of time here talking about joy, choice, limits, sufficiency and existence being an extension–do you notice a pattern? We would suggest here, dear friends, that if you were to observe yourselves very carefully and observe the choices that you allow yourselves to make in your existence, you would observe the limits to which you yourselves choose to impose on the joy of your existence. You would observe the degree to which you limit your joy of existence.

Now, existence itself, in its natural state, is a state of absolute joy, we assure you. Existence itself was not intended to be painful, sorrowful, damaging, hurtful, reducing, denigrating or denying. You did not create existence with the intent to experience pain and sorrow, we assure you. Many individuals believe that, when they incarnated, they had a certain direction of existence—to experience pain and sorrow. They see it as karma or karmic reaction to their existence. And as a result, they choose to accept pain, sorrow, hurt, denigration, and denial in their existence, for after all, this is payback for karma.

And we would suggest that this is poppycock, sheer poppycock! There is no such thing as an automatic payback. There is no such thing as an automatic denigration of your existence. There is no such thing as an automatic denial of yourselves. No such thing as an automatic reduction of joy in your existence. There is, however, such a thing as choosing to reduce the joy of your existence. And if you choose to believe that it is necessary for you to reduce your existence in order to experience the experience of payback, we assure you, you do so out of joy. You do so from a joy of love.

Some would suggest that if that's the case, why would we even bother? And we would suggest, absolutely, why bother? Why bother reducing your existence in order to experience pain, sorrow, reduction, denial, denigration or karmic payback? We assure you, there is no reason that can be described as valid for doing so. There is reason that can be justified on the basis of ego-personality, for it perceives itself as "less than" and therefore it can justify itself in a number of different ways. But we assure you, regardless of how you perceive the justification, the only validity of the choice of reduction is that you choose to do so, and as a result, you choose to do so out of joy.

Think about this. Here you are all standing in a group, each one of you flagellating each other and saying, "Oh joy, isn't this wonderful. Hit me again please. Oh joy, isn't this wonderful. One more time, I really want to feel this one. Oh joy, isn't this wonderful, do it again. Do it again and do it again." We would suggest that this would make a good scene in a comedy, but not much more than that.

There is no need to deny and denigrate yourselves. Far from it. Therefore, why not instead stand in a circle or a group and appreciate each other and say, "Oh joy, love me some more. Oh joy, compliment me more. Oh joy, appreciate me more. Oh joy, do it again and again and again." Both are joy. The choice is yours as to which one you would like. We would suggest that of greater expansion of existence is to recognize that because you can choose any–and we do say *any*–aspect of existence, why not choose an aspect that is loving, supportive and expansive to the self as opposed to a circumstance or situation that denies and denigrates the self?

Now, at the beginning of this session we discussed the fact that certain choices were made consciously from an ego-personality, subconsciously and unconsciously. And as a result, we're suggesting that you begin to recognize the degree to which you can command yourselves, in your existence, to choose to your benefit, to choose to reflect the joy of your existence, to choose to allow your existence to be a reflection of the joy of your existence. You can do so. But it requires a willingness to do so consciously.

Now, some would argue that if every choice in our existence had to be conscious, you would be overwhelmed. After all, if choice is made every moment of existence, how can you be conscious of every choice? And we would suggest, who needs to? The point is *begin.* Don't sit there and say, "I can't do it, it's too much." And therefore you sit with arms crossed, simply waiting for existence to happen to you. And then you say, "See there, I proved to myself again what a lousy life I have."

We would suggest, choose and choose again and choose again, and each choice that you make, be conscious of why you choose to make that choice as best as you can. For we assure you, if you are conscious in the moment of why you make a choice, even though the result of that choice may not be what your ego-personality would anticipate, you will maintain a degree of consciousness that will expand, and the joy in your existence will expand. You will find yourselves leading a joyful, empowered existence that will move you from perspective to perspective, from circumstance to situation, and allow you to choose the direction of your existence to your benefit.

Think of it. It's the equivalent of someone not

knowing how to swim, deciding to go into the water and saying to themselves, "I don't know quite how to swim, but I will try." After one stroke, two strokes, the nose goes under the water, the eyes fall under, the breathing comes in, water goes into the lungs, the person gags and says, "There you go, that's it; I'm not going to do this again." And as a result, for the remainder of her existence she only ventures into the water no deeper than her big toe for fear of gagging, regardless of the fact that her mouth is not near her big toe. But this is what she chooses. For after all, if she were to trip and fall, her mouth might be in the water, and she might gag.

The alternative is to be conscious of why you allowed the nose to go under the water, why the mouth went under, why the choice was made to attempt something that, at that point, you weren't ready to do. Then you can choose not to fear the experience, not to limit the experience and make choices that would eventually lead you to become a great swimmer. That's the alternative.

Your existence is the same. You can spend your time making one choice and letting the rest remain in a subconscious and unconscious perspective as a result of created belief structures–which, in effect, will limit your existence–or you can begin to make choices consciously, recognizing that every time you choose, you do so out of joy, and therefore that joy manifests itself in your existence. The more you choose consciously, the more conscious joy you bring to your existence, the more conscious expansion you bring to your existence.

Have you ever seen an individual who chooses everything consciously? There isn't a happier individual. Why? Because they choose everything, and they know they choose everything. They choose the drink they're going to have for breakfast, what they're going to eat, how their body is going to feel. They choose the clothes they're going to wear; in fact, they even choose the underwear they wear. They choose the make-up, the hair, the style, the color; they choose the car; they choose the job; they choose the environment; they choose their friends; they choose their relationships; they choose the circumstances of their existence. And as a result, they are joyful and they manifest it.

And when the choice brings sorrow and pain, they are joyful at recognizing that they have brought to their consciousness an awareness of a choice made unconsciously and subconsciously. As a result, they can expand that existence by then moving that choice to the conscious perspective. And they choose to do so; and again more joy expands their existence. Look around, you will find these individuals. We assure you, they exist. They're all around you. There aren't many, but they are all around you. Each one that you observe, regardless of who it is you observe, you can observe the joy they have in their existence, if you choose. However, we assure you that if you don't have a great deal of joy in your existence, you will choose not to observe a joyful person. Why would you choose to observe a joyful person to remind you of what you don't have? Some would because they like to be reminded of their lack. Most would not, but there are some who would. Some like to know that they are "less than" and like to be reminded of their perceptions of "less than." But it is all a perception–that's all it is–and the perception is an illusion.

Joy, however, is not an illusion. Joy is the constant permeating all of your existence. As a result, regardless of what you choose, regardless of the circumstances under which the choice is made–regardless of whether it be conscious, subconscious or unconscious in relation to the ego-personality–we assure you that each choice that you make, you do so out of joy. Therefore, observe the degree of joy that you have, that you are experiencing in your existence, and you will observe the degree to which you consciously are allowing yourselves to choose.

We assure you, you have joy in your existence. Regardless of whether the choice is conscious or unconscious, the joy exists. However, to observe the joy, you must then observe the conscious perspective of the choice made. And then, dear friends, it would be the equivalent of standing under Niagara Falls when someone had dammed it, and all of a sudden the dam opens on top of you. We assure you, the water will rush over you, take you, carry you and give you the greatest ride of your life. Now, this isn't something to be afraid of. Some people would say, "But all that water will kill me." We assure you, it will not. It will bring you on the greatest ride of your existence. It will give you the greatest joy, the greatest experience, the greatest expansion; it will move you to expand your existence beyond the limits you've set for yourselves. And then, dear friends, the joy will so fill your heart that you will choose to share it with others. Not just with one or two or three, but with so many that eventually they will laugh at the giddiness of the joy within you.

Think of it this way: When you walk down the street, and someone goes by you laughing, and you wonder why, it's because he perceives the joy in you. Joy, in effect, is contagious. It brings about a certain giddiness, a certain lightness of heart to individuals. Joy is that which resonates with the heart chakra. It is the self-love. No one can resist self-love–no one. Not even the most closed-off person could resist self-love. Now, we didn't say that he/she wouldn't react to it differently. We said she couldn't resist it.

Therefore, give yourselves the opportunity to recognize the joy that you have of your existence. And when, as a result of a choice, a certain circumstance or situation occurs that to you is defined or judged as being hurtful, sorrowful or harmful to your existence, observe the joy with which you made that choice. Observe how much self-love you have that allowed you to make that choice in your existence. And recognize that, though you may not perceive the interconnection of that choice to the joy of the totality of existence, there is an interconnection. And that a choice made at any moment of existence can manifest itself at any other moment of existence.

As a result, be willing to experience the joy of your existence. "That Which You Choose, You Do So Out of Joy." Dear friends, there is not a more powerful statement–other than the other four that we gave you, which are equally powerful. There is no more powerful statement than these. Explore, experience, expand and enjoy.

Additional Comments

On the flow of energy or movement that the defining statements create

If you follow each statement from the first to the second, through the third, the fourth and then the fifth, you will recognize that the focus of the statements will move the energy of consciousness, of expansion within yourselves from an outward-perspective to an inward perspective. Now, the reason that the first and the fifth are outward perspective statements is that they allow you to recognize that aspect of yourselves that you project. The second and the third are definitive inward statements that allow you to recognize that which is the source. The fourth itself is an inward and outward statement, a balanced statement that brings about to you a certain awareness of the movement of the energy of inward and outward.

Also, recognize another correlation here—and this is an interesting correlation for all of you. None of you have picked up on it. The first statement is "Existence Is But an Extension of Yourself." And where does existence come from but the first chakra, the survival chakra? In the second statement, "I Am Sufficient," sufficiency applies not simply to the first, but to the second and the third. And to the fourth, however, mostly to the first, second and third. The third statement, "I Am Limitless; My Choices Reflect My Limitlessness," is an expansion of the third and the fourth chakra, and an expression of the fifth. The fourth statement, "That Which I Am Is That Which You Are, and That Which You Are Is That Which I Am," is a good, well-balanced statement, wouldn't you say? A focal point where that which came before balances with that which came after. Therefore, it is equivalent to the fourth chakra itself. As to the fifth statement, "That Which You Choose, You Do So Out of Joy,"—where do you choose from but the fourth, fifth and sixth chakras? Interesting correlation that none of you chose to observe. And yet, you did so out of joy.

Now, viewed from that perspective, we assure you that you will recognize that the validity of the statements we've made is to bring about not simply an expansion of consciousness (for we could have done so differently), but also an expansion of awareness and a movement of energy that will allow the healing of the consciousness to take place. Once you apply these statements in your existence and choose to observe yourselves in relation to these statements in your existence, the choices you will make will alter and shift, and the joy of your existence will expand. That will eventually lead us to the sixth statement. No, we're not giving it to you now. Not yet.

We're suggesting that as you work with these statements, as you bring them into your life, you're also expanding that chakra to which they pertain. That you are, in effect, bringing more energy into that chakra, and as a result, expanding your existence. Interesting, isn't it? And then you move outward and inward, inward and outward. And so you thread a needle from the first chakra to the second, to the third, the fourth, the fifth, the sixth, and with the sixth statement to the seventh chakra.

Now, we gave you a hint, but you didn't pick up on it. We expressed how the five statements related to the six chakras, did we not? And what was the example of threading the needle? Did it go only to six chakras? No, it went from the sixth statement to the seventh chakra. Interesting. There is your hint.

Congratulations. You've now passed grade one. Move on to grade two. We did so, dear friends, because during the discussion period [at the channeling session] each and every one of you questioned how to be observant. Did you not? You were wondering how to expand your observation in your existence.

True? Yet none of you observed the statement we made. You listened to the parts you wanted to listen to, for we had discussed at great length the five defining statements and how they related to the six chakras. But none of you was willing to listen to the statement we made about threading the needle. And that was because none of you want to spoil your fun—the fun of not knowing.

Think of it this way: If you were to observe that the sixth statement will relate to the seventh chakra—which, of course, we've told you now, so you've observed it at this point—if you were to have observed this previously, you would have found yourselves disappointed. For then you would have known, and the anticipation would have been eliminated. Had we told you earlier that we were going to do this, all of you would have been totally disappointed. Especially this one. The anticipation he has experienced has given him such pleasure and such joy that, we assure you, it will be hard to repeat for at least another two days.

On using observation to expand the perception of choice

You can expand the perception of choice by choosing to observe. Whether it be conscious, unconscious or subconscious, we assure you, choose to observe and you will observe. Choose to observe the observation.

We would suggest, dear friends, there's nothing difficult here. Each and every one of you is telling yourselves that this is the most difficult session you've ever encountered. Dear friends, it's not. In fact, it's the simplest. Choose. That's all, choose. And observe how the choice reflects the joy of your existence. The observation expands the choice. The choice precedes everything. Choose. Choose and then, we assure you, choose to observe. You must choose first. You chose to exist; that was one of the beginning choices. That was a choice, now choose to observe. And use observation as a tool to expand your awareness of existence so that in the expansion of the awareness of existence you can then choose differently.

This isn't difficult, dear friends. In fact, if there were a number of five-year-olds in this particular room, they would tell you that it is quite easy—simply choose. You complicate it, because in your existence you tend to view each choice as needing justification. Don't justify. Simply choose. Have you ever seen a five-year-old? We assure you, it doesn't take them long to change their minds. They choose and they choose, and then they choose again. And when they're finished with what they've chosen, they choose differently. They don't spend time justifying it to themselves. We assure you, it doesn't take long. In fact, there are a number of individuals who get frustrated by five-year-olds because they don't play the game of justification. Stop playing this game with yourselves. Stop giving yourselves the necessity to justify your choices. You spend so much energy justifying your choices that you give yourselves very little time to choose. Choose and know that you can change the choice.

View it from this perspective: Take a glass of rum. You know that if you take an ounce and a half of rum in six ounces of cola, the chances are good that it will affect the body. True? Good alcohol, especially good, aged rum, will affect the body very well. True? In fact, it might even give you a little buzz, and for some individuals, it will make you totally drunk. Therefore, you choose to know that alcohol will affect the body. But you can also choose to deny it and then choose to experience alcohol.

Is one choice more valid than the other? No. Is one choice more beneficial than the other? From one perspective, the answer is no. But from the perspective of judgment, it's yes. And as a result, when you make the choice and you judge the result of that choice, some individuals would say, "Being sober is a better experience. Therefore, I choose not to drink." We assure you, there are many others who would say that having a buzz on is even more fun. "Let's choose to do it again." And some would say, "Being totally drunk is the greatest experience. Let's remain in that state always."

No one choice is more valid than the other. It is simply based on the choice of the experience. That each choice is based on the perspective of joy is true. However, if you view your existence from the perspective of joy, you will recognize the degree of joy you bring into your existence. Is the drunk more or less joyful than the sober individual? We assure you, in some cases the drunk is more joyful than the sober individual. For the sober individual looks at the drunk and wishes that he could be as oblivious as the drunk.

Do you see? There is no judgment here. Set aside judgment and simply choose the experience. In some cases, you will recognize that there is no need to experience getting drunk. You've done this before. You know the result, and so you choose not to experience that result. This doesn't make that choice less valid or more valid; it simply makes it different. And based on the circumstances that you find yourselves in, drunk may not be the answer.

There is a good television clip in which Mr. Bean stands in front of the Queen, drunk, trying to raise his fly. Unfortunately, his finger gets caught. Drunk on that occasion could have certain repercussions. His finger could get cut off. However, sober on that occasion would prevent him from putting his finger in his fly, wouldn't it? Either way, there is a great deal of joy as a result of the experience.

Now, some of you might think that if you observe your previous choice, then your next choice can perhaps be made from a more expanded awareness, which is true from one perspective. But even within the concept of expanded awareness is a perspective of judgment. We would suggest that it is simply made from a different awareness. And here, dear friends, we are beginning to shift you as a group. We are moving you from the perspective of judgment. And we did make this observation so that you would observe it carefully.

This is because it's time, because you're ready. All of you have observed judgment to a degree in your existence, and as a result, you're now ready to observe the extent of the judgment in your existence. You even judge the expansion of your consciousness. Any type of labeling is not necessarily judgment. However, from certain perspectives, because of the limitations of the English language, certain words must be used in order to express a certain concept. As a result of this, we use those words. However, if you view the words carefully, expansion of consciousness is a nonjudgmental concept.

But when you apply it in your existence, and you view yourselves and measure yourselves on the basis of expansion of consciousness, you judge yourselves. Notice how each and every one of you, when we speak of expansion of consciousness, look at yourselves inwardly and say, "I'm not quite there yet." True? And how many of you look at the one next to you and say, "I wonder if she's there yet?" Most of you do this, true? Isn't that judgment, dear friends?

But expansion of consciousness is not a concept based on judgment. In and of itself. It's how you apply the concept in your existence that creates judgment. Therefore, don't judge yourselves. Don't judge the judgment. Simply allow yourselves to expand, knowing that that which you are–and we will repeat here, listen carefully—*that which you are is sufficient.* It isn't necessary to judge.

However, the concept to expand your consciousness has validity. To allow yourselves to move to a perspective whereby the consciousness is more aware of existence, more observant of existence, has a greater perspective of existence—that has validity. But to judge yourselves on the basis that you're an expanded consciousness and he's not? We would suggest here, dear friends, that the ones who judge aren't as expanded as they think they are. And that was a good lesson on judgment.

On accepting the so-called negative choices we've made without beating ourselves up over them

Recognize that there are no negative choices. You see a choice as a negative, and you judge it. You assign it a value. You say that this choice denigrates my existence, denies it; and as a result, you constantly denigrate yourselves for denigrating, for choosing a denigrating choice. You judge yourselves for judging. We would suggest that you give yourselves the permission to recognize that each choice is simply a perspective of a benefit. In fact, if you choose, dear friends, view it as a degree of benefit. Therefore, don't judge yourselves for making a choice that has a lesser degree of benefit than another choice. Simply see that each choice has a degree of benefit, and accept and enjoy the degree of benefit that you choose. Then give yourselves permission to change the choice. The reason you judge the choices that you make, and the reason that you judge yourselves for judging the choices you make, is that you don't give yourselves permission to alter your choices.

You can overcome the fear that the choice you make is not the right choice by recognizing that it is only an illusion. Fear itself, dear friends, is created by the ego as an illusion to maintain the perspective of self-control. Fear itself is not real. What would happen if you were to take responsibility for your choices? What would occur? Would you cast off feet of clay? Would you cease to exist? Would you remove yourselves from any connection to God/Goddess/The All That Is?

Therefore, what's to fear? You would have to say, "I did this. I chose. I am responsible for me." But the result of making that statement would not shatter your existence. It would not alter your existence to the point of elimination of existence. But it would alter the existence. From one perspective, it would alter it and allow you to make another choice. That way, you would say, "I chose this," true. But it would not eliminate the existence. It would not dissipate the existence. And that's the fear. The fear says that if you choose to accept responsibility for your choice, then your existence will cease to exist as it is. And from one perspective, that is correct; to accept responsibility for your choices will alter your existence. But you will not cease to exist. The fear is the illusion, dear friends. See it for what it is.

When what seems like a right choice turns out not to be, it only turns out to be wrong because you judge the results of the choice. And the reason you judge the results of that choice is because of a limited perspective of the choice.

An example: An individual recognizes that she is in an untenable situation at work. She cannot possibly continue, she must leave. And as a result of this, she decides to leave work and find herself another job. The other job pays the equivalent amount of money, has the same benefits, and nothing much has changed. But then the individual finds out that shortly after she left her old job, everybody got a $10,000 raise. The individual kicks herself in the butt for having made that choice. However, at the time the choice was made, the reason the choice was made was because that individual felt unempowered, and she therefore empowered herself by making a different choice. That individual would then judge the result on the basis of hindsight, on the basis of having missed something–$10,000 is, after all, a lot of money. However, the circumstances of the new choice have yet to be explored. In the meantime, judgment is applied on the basis of a limited perspective.

On relationships and making choices when other people are involved

We focused on the perspective that "That Which You Choose, You Do So Out of Joy" so you could observe the outward and the inward. You can point the finger and say to another, "That which you choose, you do so out of joy. Not me, I don't do it out of joy at all. You do, but not me." Or you could say, "That which you choose, you do so out of joy, just the same as me. Aren't you lucky?"

As a result, it's irrelevant who makes the choice. The result is that you are placed in a circumstance where, as a result of your choice, you choose to be interrelated to the choice of another, that's true. And the other also chooses to place himself/herself in the same circumstance whereby that choice will affect him. But it is his choice. He has free will, you have free will. He could choose differently, and if he chose differently, then another would choose to be in that circumstance. In other words, it isn't a given that the same person will always place himself there.

People will often go into relationships and say to themselves, "I choose you. You must be the chosen one. You must be my soul mate, you must be my twin flame, you must be the one that I would be with." And we would suggest, that in one of a thousand, yes. One of a million, possibly. It is only that that one made the correct choices in the proper way that allowed her to place herself in that circumstance at that moment. She isn't the only one. She is the only one who chose, and that's the difference.

View existences past and future in relation to this existence. You will recognize that, many times when we speak to individuals, they have had more than one mate over many existences. Why? Because different individuals choose different experiences at different times. As a result, you might meet another individual at a different time because of the choices you make and the choices that individual made that brought you together. Are you interrelated? From one perspective, yes. Have you had previous lives? From one perspective, yes. Will you have more? From one perspective, yes. Will they always be the same? No.

View this one and dear Maggie. With your permission, dear Maggie, we will use you and this one as an example. Both these two individuals have had many lives together. In fact, as we've suggested to them previously, they've been together 3,472 lifetimes, of which, in 2,893, they were primary mates. However, no one has asked how many lifetimes did each of them have? Separately, individually, they had many, many more beyond that. As a result, they've had many, many other mates. Different choices. In this one's lifetime and in dear Maggie's lifetime in this very existence, both of them have had many other mates. Yet they chose to be together.

It isn't a given that you are born, you live, you mate, you die. That isn't how existence works. In some existences, yes, this is true. Because of circumstances, because of societal circumstances, you choose one mate, and that's it. Many other times, circumstances bring about the choice of many other mates. Yet each one different, brought together at that very moment.

If this one had made different choices, he would have never have met dear Maggie. And if dear Maggie had made different choices, she would never have met this one. Both made certain choices that brought them together, that led them together. Could they have chosen differently? Absolutely. They had free will. They chose not to. They chose to choose in the way that they chose in order to bring them together—and figure that one out! But they did. And had they chosen differently, they wouldn't have been together at this point in time. At another point in time, yes. But time doesn't exist. Therefore, it is irrelevant whether it is in this lifetime or another lifetime. They would have come together at some point. And then from your perspective, when you ask us questions about lifetime, or their perspective, when they asked us about their lifetimes, we can answer them on the basis of total lifetimes, total existence.

There was a probability that those choices would lead them together. That was a choice that soul-essence made from that perspective. The probability existed. But because of free will and free choice of ego-personality, it required a willingness on both their parts to make the choices to bring themselves together. Had Réné done things differently or had Maggie done things differently, they would have found different mates. And that which they are now would not be. And we would have waited, for we ourselves also form part of them, as they form part of ourselves. However, we did prod both of them a little.

We can only guide and suggest though; it was still their choice. Each and every one of you has guides, has suggestions given to you, but you have the free will and free choice to observe those suggestions and to follow them or set them aside. And that's the beauty of choice. For in truth, regardless of what you choose, you do so out of joy. Fascinating, isn't it?

But again, it is choice. As a result, there is an interrelationship, yes. But it's an interrelationship that's separate from one another, free of one another, both making the choices that led them to this particular experience. And if we do say so, both made choices that have expanded their existence.

From that perspective, there's no such thing as coincidence in your existence. For with each and every individual you meet, there is a purpose for it based on choices that you've made. You can affect or draw into your lives relationships based on how you feel about yourselves and your own self-love. The more you expand your self-love, the more you can choose to expand that self-love through relationships. And as a result, the more joy you bring into your existence.

It's like being in a police lineup–ten men all lined up in a row. You're standing in front, and you have a choice. If you choose one way, you get choice number one. Choose another way, poor fellow, number three. Choice number five, oh well, not as good as you thought. Choice number ten, very abusive. Choice number six, now there's a loving guy. Depending on the choices you make, you get to pick one, two, three, or more, in fact, if you choose. And there's another ten, and a hundred, and a thousand behind them, waiting to be chosen as well, if the choices come together.

Now, we're not suggesting here that choosing more than one mate over a lifetime is necessarily more expansive than staying with one. It depends on the circumstances of the relationship and the circumstances of the choices you make in your existence. If as a result of certain choices you've made, you find yourself in a very constricting, a very limiting, a very damaging, hurtful, denigrating, denying relationship, and then as a result of certain other choices, you choose to view yourself in a loving way, then to remain in that relationship would not honor the new choices you've made. To honor those new choices requires either that the relationship shifts or that the relationship changes. And as a result of this, it then requires other individuals to choose expansions. You make new choices, but you must honor that which you choose. For that which you choose is that which you choose out of joy.

So it's not a given that as you grow, the relationship will change or the relationship will end, and as a result, a new mate will be taken. It is not a given. For often the other individual in the relationship is also willing to alter and shift and grow as well. And so two individuals, choosing to grow together, also choose to stay together. But if one chooses to expand his/her consciousness and self-love in such a way that the choices he makes are more loving to himself and the other chooses not to, then we assure you, the relationship has no foundation, no basis for existence. And then a choice is made to review the existence of the relationship.

On experiencing pain as a choice

Even pain is a choice, we assure you. You have had many lifetimes in which you flagellated yourselves consistently using a leather whip. You beat yourselves until your skin was literally cut and you were bleeding–and you enjoyed every moment of it. You don't use the whip anymore. That would be too sexual. However, recognize that you do make choices that are, in effect, the equivalent of flagellation. Each and every one of you does the same. This isn't rocket science, dear friends. Quite simply, each and every one of you, at this point in your existence, still makes choices that denigrate yourselves. And you do so because you do not perceive yourselves as being deserving of a different choice, as having the value and the validity to make a different choice.

This is key to each and every one of you. If you were to see a three- to five-year-old girl crying in the middle of the street, bleeding kneecap, bleeding arm, tears running down from the eyes through the mud–for she was dirty, she'd been playing in the mud–what would you do? You would love her, wouldn't you? You would want to protect her, you would want to care for that child. You'd nurture that child. You'd give that child love. True?

That child is you, dear friends. Inside of you, you are bleeding and cut and sore and crying, and yet each and every day, you choose not to love yourselves. Not to give yourselves the nurturing and the love that you so clearly cry out for. Why? We assure you, no one else is viewing that child inside of you. They see you as adults. They see you as certain individuals, certain perspectives, but none of you are willing to look inside and give yourselves the love. We assure you, each and every one of you is a young child crying for love, pained, hurt, wanting to be hugged and held. In fact, think of it this way: See yourselves as an infant looking for a breast to feed on. What is more beautiful, it has been said, than the Madonna feeding the child? You are the child and you are the Madonna. Regardless of whether you are male or female, you are the Madonna. Feed the child inside of you, nurture and love it. Give it nourishment, give it love. Give yourselves love, give yourselves nourishment. And then observe the joy that comes from doing so.

Have you ever seen the eyes of a young infant after it's suckled on its mother's breasts? Look into those eyes. We assure you, you will see not only a burping child, you will see satisfaction, you will see joy and contentment–and a good strong burp. But there is joy and contentment. Why? Because the child is nurtured, it is full. Give this to yourselves. Now we're not suggesting that you contort yourselves and suckle on your own breasts, but that you give yourselves love. Make choices that reflect to you the extent to which you love yourselves. And then love yourselves more.

We often suggest to individuals that they see themselves as a cup, and that which fills the cup is love. If you see yourselves as only half full, the most you can do is half fill another cup. If you are full, the most you can do is fill one other cup. We suggest that you so fill yourselves with love that you overflow, and let the overflow fill all the other cups. What's the overflow, dear friends, but joy–joy! And the love in the cup, that's the nurturing.

From this moment forward, view every decision you have through the filter of the illusion, or the perspective, or the imagination of you as the young infant suckling the very love of life. Your mother's breast is life; suckle on it. Get it until you are so full that you are content and joyful. Choose. Use anything you choose. But ask yourselves as you make the choice, what choice would you make for this young child, for this young infant?

CHAPTER SIX

All That I Am Is Love; All That You Are Is Love

The Sixth Defining Statement

This is the sixth and final defining statement that we shall give you at this point with regards to your existence, dear friends. Let us review before going into this. The first defining statement, "Existence Is But an Extension of Yourself"; the second, "I Am Sufficient"; the third, "I Am Limitless; My Choices Reflect My Limitlessness"; the fourth, "That Which You Are Is That Which I Am, and That Which I Am Is That Which You Are"; the fifth defining statement, "That Which You Choose, You Do So Out of Joy." And now the sixth, "All That I Am Is Love; All That You Are Is Love."

These defining statements will assist you in recognizing the extension of your existence at this particular point in your existence. If you choose, you can use these defining statements to expand your existence, to move beyond that which you are. Each statement has brought you to a certain point of understanding, a certain point of recognition, a certain point of awareness. However, the key to recognize is that the last defining statement will encompass the other five.

Let's begin with the part of the statement that says, "All That I Am Is Love." First, the word "all." We did not say "part"; we did not say "a parcel"; we did not say "this part" or "that part"; we did not say "the good side"; we didn't say "the acceptable side", we didn't say "the part that interacts with others," "the part that is thoughtful," "the part that is compassionate," "the part that is courageous," "the part that is empowered." We said "all." "All That I Am Is Love"—the "I" being yourself, of course.

What this statement basically says is that every aspect of that which is that which you are, is, in effect, love—regardless of what part you're looking at, regardless of the aspect, regardless of the perspective, regardless of any portion of the self, how it's perceived, how it's acted upon, how it's manifested. "All That I Am Is Love" is a very, very strong statement. There is no exclusion. There is no part of yourself that is not love.

To define love in this particular statement would be to state that that which you are, in effect, is energy manifest of God/Goddess/The All That Is—pure love extended. Therefore, every aspect of yourself is love:

the physical, the mental, the emotional, the spiritual, the conscious, the subconscious, the superconscious, the high conscious, the high self, the low self, the mid-self, the soul-essence, the ego-personality, the incarnation, the extension of yourself. However you wish to describe that which you are, dear friends, every aspect of that which you are is love.

In effect, when you apply this statement by stating it within your existence, by making the statement, "All That I Am Is Love," at that point, you are empowering yourselves to perceive that which you are, which is love. Every choice that you make, every decision that you choose, every opportunity that you find yourselves faced with, every circumstance of existence in which you place yourselves, every aspect of your existence, however it's manifested, can be defined by the statement, "All That I Am Is Love." There isn't one part that can be set aside.

Now, let's go back the fifth statement, "That Which You Choose, You Do So Out of Joy." Joy is an extension of love. Therefore, the fifth is an extension of the sixth. The first statement, "Existence Is But an Extension of Yourself"–if you choose, you could say existence is but an extension of "myself." However you choose to describe that, existence is an extension of love.

For those of you who have spent time meditating, pondering, reflecting on certain aspects of these particular statements that we've given you, you'll recognize that every statement (however it's been said, however it's been described) comes, in effect, from the sixth, which is why we haven't given you the sixth prior to this particular point. True, we gave you the first five, and we gave them to you at the same period of time. And, from one perspective, we allowed you to reflect on each one. From another perspective, you chose to. However, the key to recognize is that the sixth could not be given, because the sixth is, in effect, the creator of the first five.

Now, this seems a little backward, some would say. After all, why would the end be the creator of the beginning, of what came before? And we would suggest to you, dear friends, that it is very appropriate to your existence. For in truth, you perceive yourselves as an end. Yet you create your own beginnings. And from that perspective, recognize that that which you are now is but a reflection of the creative energy that you've chosen to manifest. Therefore, the end is the beginning and the beginning is the end.

You are not a culmination. You are, in truth, part of the process. As such, you reflect the energy of love that you are. You are entities, dear friends—energy entities, from one perspective. That you perceive yourselves as having physical bodies and being physical entities is a choice you make. But you are, from our perspective, energy entities. As such, you are the creators of your own existence. As such, you are the manifestors of your own love. And as such, therefore, you are love.

If you but recognize this, dear friends, then you recognize and give yourselves permission to observe the extent of your own existence—of the breadth and depth of your existence. "All That I Am Is Love." Some would say that that statement can be ascribed to the Nazarene, to Buddha or to Mohammed, but not to yourselves; for, after all, you are not at their level. And we would suggest, poppycock!

In truth, dear friends, there is no difference between yourselves, the Nazarene, Buddha and Mohammed. It is just that at the particular moment in time when they chose to manifest themselves, perceptions were different and altered. You are the same. Perceptions are different, yes, but you are the same. You are the same energy. You are love.

Notice we said, "All That I Am." That includes your soul-essence. If you use the perspective that we've suggested of thirty-two dimensions of reality with God/Goddess/The All That Is on the thirty-second dimension, it suggests that every soul-essence that is an extension of God/Goddess/The All That Is, regardless of the dimension that it is on, that forms part of that which you are—all of that is love. "All That I Am Is Love."

Now, on to the next part of the statement, "All That You Are Is Love." We could have said, "All That I Am Is Love" is the sixth defining statement, and that would have been it. We gave the next part to you for you to reflect the movement of energy, the yin and the yang of the universe. That that which is is that which comes; that which is is that which was as it moves, as it flows. As there is an ebb and flow, so is there a relation. There is a left to a right. There is a right to a left. There is an up to a down. There is an in to an out. Everything is in balance.

If we had said only the statement, "All That I Am Is Love," it would have been out of balance. For in truth, all that you are is love. However you say it, whether it be ourselves, whether it be yourselves–regardless of who speaks the phrase–we assure you, it applies. Therefore, if you were to repeat after us and say, "All That I Am Is Love; All That You Are Is Love," in speaking to ourselves, we would assure you, we would agree. We are love, the same as you. And you are love, the same as us. Manifested differently, true. But still love energy. The energy that cannot be measured by your scientists. They've yet to discover a methodology for measuring love energy.

Oh, they can measure electricity, they can measure microwaves, they can measure magnetic energy, they can measure light energy. But they cannot yet measure love energy. They will, but not yet. And they cannot do so because they choose not to perceive the universe as being created by, moving through and being manifested as a result of love energy.

They perceive it in different terms. Some describe it as universal energy. It is a way of describing love energy. We assure you, there is nothing simplistic and nothing reduced about love energy. Universal energy is mankind's way of attempting to reduce that which they do not understand. It is a term that ascribes to universality, true. But in the usage of the term, many individuals use it as a way of reducing that which they perceive as love energy. "Why describe something as love energy, which is a very powerful word? Let's reduce it to universal energy, which is an acceptable word to everyone."

And so the psychology, the belief structures of reduction, still applies to how you describe and manifest yourselves. Yet, that which you are, dear friends, is nothing short of love. It's nothing else. You aren't skin and bones. You aren't cellular structure. You aren't DNA. You aren't genes interacting with each other. You aren't sperm and egg, fertilized. You aren't a mind; you aren't a brain. You are all of those things, true–but you are more. You are love.

Now, there's no way for us to describe this any differently, dear friends. We can provide you with a perspective of that which you perceive as love. We can move you beyond your perception. We can extend our energy such that you resonate with the energy within yourselves that is an energy of love. And we will do this before the end of this very session–and we assure you, you will get that love energy, for we will include it into these words. However, regardless of how you choose to perceive and observe, you are love energy.

Now, what does this mean, in practical terms? View

it from this perspective: You're the type of individual who gets up in the morning at six o'clock, rushes to get yourself shaved and dressed–if you're female, then perhaps only dressed, not shaved–and you get yourself ready to go to work, get the children off to school, get yourself rushing to work. You envelop yourself, focus yourself into your daily activity at work for eight to ten hours a day, then you rush home, grab some supper, and hopefully spend a few minutes of quality time with your children. Get them to bed and maybe give yourself a moment or two with your spouse, your mate or by yourself, and then you rush to get to bed, to get to sleep, only to start the process all over again. And you do this five days a week. And you rush through those five days so that you can get two days to yourself–these are *your* two days, not for anyone else.

So what do you do on those two days? You rush to go out and do the grocery shopping, you rush to go out and fix the house, you rush to go out and visit family that you wouldn't visit otherwise. You rush to fulfill all the things that you perceive to be obligations in your life. You rush here, you rush there. And so your life is fulfilled. Or so you think.

And you see yourself as being complete and whole. You're satisfied. After all, you have a good spouse, you have the national average of 2.2 children, you have a good house, two cars, two TV sets, a good stereo system. You have a little bit of money in the bank, and like most other individuals in North American society, you have a lot of debt. And you feel comfortable, for you are part of life. After all, isn't everybody the same? And you look around you when you drive in the morning on a highway or a road, and you look at everyone beside you, and they're all looking the same. They all have a coffee to their lips, bleary-eyed, some are putting on their make-up, some are shaving, some are reading magazines while they're sitting in traffic, waiting for the traffic to move. The odd one is working on his computer with his fax machine beside him in the car.

And you think that life is wonderful, life is grand. True, you get your two weeks per year. After all, you've invested fifty weeks of your life into a company, and the company graciously says to you, "Thank you for having given us fifty weeks. We'll give you two so that you can go out and relax." And off you go. You rush like heck to get ready to go on your vacation. You do everything you can to ensure that everything is taken care of while you're gone for your two weeks. Because if something happens while you're gone, your company, those individuals around you, may doubt your validity and your abilities. So you do everything you can to ensure that your two weeks are well taken care of, and then you rush to get to the cottage or to get to wherever you're going for your vacation. Some individuals rush for two weeks, driving here, driving there, trying to see as much as they can and do as much as they can within that time. You try to cram ten years of life into two weeks, because that's all you have. And you think, "Life is wonderful. Life is grand." You live from day to day, waiting for weekends—waiting for long weekends especially, when you can get an extra day's holiday where you don't have to go to work.

And the odd time, you sit and finally say, "I've had enough." And on those days, you rush like heck to go to the movie theater, or to go to the video store and rent videos before everybody else does so that you can go home and watch the movies in peace. You order pizza or chicken, good food that'll nourish the body. Food that you *think* will nourish the body, but which, in effect, poisons your body. But you don't see it that way; you think you're being nourished. And there you are, sitting content and wondering why you're accumulating weight, sitting in front of a TV, eating pizza and watching a good movie. But in the meantime, if you sit and reflect, every moment of your life is a rush.

Now, some would say that this is a great way of living, for after all, you live on the edge when you're rushing all of your life. If every moment of your life is a rush, then it's living on the edge. It's an adrenaline rush, it's something that excites you, it's something that moves you, it makes you feel alive. And we would suggest to you, that's a heck of a way to feel alive. We would suggest to you, dear friends, that that's a very good way of feeling dead. For in truth, after you've rushed like this for fifty or sixty years, most individuals tend to die. And then when they go through the review, they wonder, "Why did I rush? I rushed to get to this point. I rushed to cast off feet of clay. Why would I do that?" But you do. And you think you've lived a good life.

Now, this is a pretty good scenario we've painted you. But this is a scenario that is exactly what it is your life is all about, we assure you. Watch. Look around you. In North American society, how many people are driving with a phone stuck to their ears? How many people are driving reading a newspaper, trying to catch up on yesterday's news because they don't have time for today? How many people are rushing to get to work and rushing to get home, rushing to go to bed, rushing to go work? Rush, rush, rush. Good life! Great life!

And those of you who are lucky get more than two weeks a year in holidays: Sometimes, you work long enough and hard enough that the company will give you reward, and after seven years, they will give you three weeks of holidays. Occasionally, in some companies, you have to work twenty years to get four weeks of holidays. And you think you've got it made. After all, isn't this what life is? What life is all about?

Here you are sitting in your wonderful house that you can't appreciate because you're so busy rushing. You sit in your wonderful car that you can't appreciate because you're so busy rushing from place to place. You're sitting in front of your television that you can't appreciate because you're so exhausted; you can barely keep your eyes open, watching the television. You have beautiful children whom you can't appreciate because they're a constant infringement upon your rushing time.

And your mates—there's another thing. You barely have time for yourself, who has time for a mate? And so you spend all of your time looking at life and saying, "Isn't this wonderful? Isn't this grand?" And you call all of this love. And you say, "But I'm in love. I love this. I love my job, I love my car, I love my work. I don't like the drive, but I love work."

And we would suggest to you, dear friends, perhaps it's time to review your definition of what you love. If this is your life and this is what you love, we assure you that there are a few treadmills we can put you on that will help you rush. We assure you, what you're doing is you're rushing to the nearest heart attack, to the nearest hospital, to the nearest kidney failure, to the nearest heart failure, to the nearest colon failure, to the nearest cancer institute. You're rushing to your deaths, and you're enjoying it. You think that life is grand, for you've accomplished something. You set out to do something, whatever that something was, and you feel that you've accomplished it. For haven't you've done exactly what everybody else is doing?

If someone took a camera and flashed it on every face that went by on the highway in the morning, we would suggest to you, dear friends, that they would be hard-pressed to find one out of 100,000 who was smiling. Most would be bleary-eyed, long-faced, angry, frustrated. And yet you think life is grand. You think your existence is wonderful.

Now, we said to you, how can this statement, "All That I Am Is Love," be used in practical terms? Let's apply that statement to your practical, everyday rushing existence. If you perceive yourself as "All That I Am," would you truly make a choice to rush to your death? Would you truly make a choice to place yourself in a line of 100,000 cars, everyone bumper to bumper, frustrated at each other, angry at each other, barely awake, gulping coffee that is really the anathema to your whole existence anyways? That will burn your insides–and we do mean it will burn then completely; it will poison you completely. If we told you that you had to stick yourself into a hot box among a thousand other hot boxes and that you had to ingest poison and enjoy the process, you would rebel. But this is what you do every day.

Therefore, if you see the statement, "All That I Am Is Love," you will recognize that every choice you make is based on love. Now the question is, how much love? What is love? For some individuals, we assure you, being on the highway at 5:30 A.M. in order to get to work by 8:30 A.M., that is love. They love that. They tell you that every morning. Ask any reporter standing on the highway interviewing people–and the reporter could probably walk faster than the cars are moving–and we assure you, they will say, "People love what they do." If they didn't, they wouldn't repeat it.

The common knowledge is that you don't repeat something that you don't love. We would suggest that's true. The key is, to which degree do you love? To which degree do you love yourselves? To which degree do you perceive yourselves as love? Do you make choices that expand your existence? Or do you make choices that contract your existence?

Now, let's go back to our scenario—and we see that we've created a great deal of humor using this scenario, but we assure you, this is true, this is real. Go back to the scenario of the individual, bleary-eyed, stumbling out of bed, head in the shower to try and open the eyes. A quick shower in the morning, gulp a cup of coffee, get dressed, jump into the car—oops, forgot the kids—quick, let's go get them. Bring them to the babysitter, the nursery school, school—wherever. "Dump them somewhere, please. Give me the chance to go to work because that is really what I want to do." And off you go, rushing to get to work. Take that scenario and then just change one choice. Change the choice of rushing to a choice of pleasurable enjoyment. Now, for some, that might then mean that to change that choice requires a change in the way they perceive work the way they perceive themselves in relation to work.

At this point, many individuals live hundreds of kilometers away from their work. Why? Because it's cheaper. They can get the house, the two cars, the two TV sets, the stereo system and of course, the 2.2 kids. They can get the North American dream. That is the dream. That is what you've been brought up on, *Leave It to Beaver* incarnate. This is the dream.

And you can get it if you live 100, 150, 200 kilometers away from your work. But that means you spend two, three, four, five, six hours per day commuting. But what's a little commuting? It's only a little bit more rush. Never mind that in that commute, there are accidents, that you increase the chances of your existence being cut short. However, it's acceptable, the odds are good. Insurance isn't too high. Houses aren't too high. Buy an old clunker, buy a cheap car that is cheap on gas. Of course, the cheap cars don't do too well in accidents; they kind of crumple. But oh well, you won't not have an accident, don't worry about it, so the thinking goes.

But if you change one choice and see yourself as love, and then choose to manifest your existence as you see yourself, then we assure you, more and more industry would be created in the area in which you live. That way, your commute is five minutes away from your home, not three or four hours. More people would choose differently. And we assure you, the old saying that, "build it and they will come," is true. If Mohammed doesn't go to the mountain, we assure you, the mountain will come to Mohammed.

If individuals, as a society, chose to love themselves and to perceive themselves as only love—which is what this statement, "All That You Are Is Love," says—then we assure you, dear friends, that the companies would not be centered as they are. It would not be you traveling to the companies; it would be the companies traveling to where the market is, to where the supply of labor is. If you made choices based upon your perception of yourselves as love, then you wouldn't be rushing fifty weeks of the year to get your two weeks of vacation and then be thankful to the company for at least allowing you two weeks off. It is the equivalent of being a slave for fifty weeks and then getting two weeks without chains. And you say, "Thank you, Master. You've given me the greatest gift you could: two weeks without chains." We assure you, that's what you're doing in terms of your existence, that's what it's all about. Every aspect of your existence is about saying, "Thank you for giving me permission to do something." But if you perceive yourselves as love, then, dear friends, it isn't about others giving you permission. It is about you giving yourselves permission; choosing for yourselves, extending your existence; choosing to extend your existence, not to contract it. There is a very practical application to your daily life.

Choose a car that is, yes, $2,000 to $3,000 more expensive than your cheap little car but that will not crumple into a thousand pieces in the event of an accident. And then you choose to give yourself an opportunity to extend your existence. Choose not to rush home every night. Choose to give yourself a bath. Choose to give yourself twenty minutes of meditation on a daily basis. Choose to give yourself time to love, make love and be loved. We assure you, dear friends, that if you begin to observe that you are love, you will choose to alter the choices in your existence to reflect that which you are.

We've often suggested to individuals–in fact, we suggest it to every individual–*observe yourself*, not from the perspective of judgment, but simply from the perspective of observation. If you do so, dear friends, you will observe that "All That You Are Is Love." And in that observation, you will begin to appreciate yourselves as love. And in that appreciation, dear friends, you will then make choices that reflect in your existence your perception of yourselves and your self-appreciation in such a way that your choices will reflect that you are love.

What does that mean? It means you will not put yourselves in jeopardy. It means you will not give another power over yourselves. It means that, when you have an opportunity, you will choose to give yourselves relaxation, you will choose not to rush. When the opportunity is there, you will choose to live a different lifestyle. You will also choose not to accept another's perspective of how your existence should be, for it is yours to choose. Choices will be made differently. Everything around you will change. Your relationship to your existence will change.

Notice how we thank dear Maggie. We do this because dear Maggie is love, as you are. When we end the sessions, we say to you all, "God's blessing." It is our way of extending our energy of love to you. For you are love, as we are. We thank you for sharing that which you are, with that which we are. "All That I Am Is Love." It could be said "All That We Are Is Love; All That You Are Is Love"–the same applies.

You are no different than we are, dear friends. You are love incarnate; you are love manifest. The choice is yours how you reflect that in your existence. We would suggest to you that of greater benefit is to choose to manifest yourselves as completely and as clearly as you can. Every choice you make–from the choice you make to get up in the morning, to the choice you make to go to bed at night, to the choice you make to stay asleep during the night–throughout your existence, throughout your daily life, is an opportunity to choose to manifest yourselves as love. Begin to observe, and you'll begin to see it.

Now, we will extend ourselves at the end of this session, but prior to doing so, we wanted to do this. The first statement, "Existence Is But an Extension of Yourself," brought you to the second statement, "I Am Sufficient." Think of it. The second statement, "I Am Sufficient," also says that "I am love, and in my love I am sufficient. My choices reflect my sufficiency, for they reflect my limitlessness, which is that which I am. I am limitless"–which is the third statement.

So therefore, if you are limitless and you make choices that reflect your limitlessness, don't they also reflect your love? Isn't this what we're talking about? If you observe yourselves as love—"All That I Am Is Love"—then you will make choices that extend your existence. And they would extend your existence, because you see yourselves as sufficient. And then, of course, once you see yourselves as sufficient, your existence becomes an extension of your sufficiency and your limitlessness and your love.

And "That Which You Are Is That Which I Am, and That Which I Am Is That Which You Are." In other words, there's no difference between you and me. There's no difference between the *I* and the *we*. There is no difference between them and us; you and them; he and she; it and all of us—there's no difference. For "That Which You Are Is That Which I Am," no different. We're not suggesting here that there are differences. We're suggesting that "That Which You Are Is That Which I Am, and That Which I Am Is That Which You Are."

And if that's the case, and I am love and all that I am is love, then that makes you "All That You Are Is Love," which of course brings you to the sixth statement. And if "All That I Am Is Love"—and that's what you are, for "That Which You Are Is That Which I Am, and That Which I Am Is That Which You Are," and "I Am Limitless, and My Choices Reflect My Limitlessness"—then that means you're limitless. And if you're limitless, that means you're sufficient because "I'm Sufficient." And if I'm sufficient and you're sufficient, that means existence is an extension of myself and yourself.

Therefore, "Existence Is an Extension of You, Me And We"–and all of us. Oh dear, this is getting complicated.

And "that which I choose, you do so out of joy?" Oh! You mean "that which you choose, that which I choose?" But if "That Which You Choose, You Do So Out of Joy," doesn't that mean "that which I choose, I do so out of joy?" Because you are me, and me are we, and you are me, and I am you. And if I am you and you are me, and I am love and you are love, and "That Which You Choose, You Do So Out of Joy," then so do I. And if joy is an extension of love, then that brings us all together. In truth, all of these statements are really just the same way of saying or different ways of saying the same thing–that "That Which You Are Is That Which I Am," and "We Are Sufficient," and "We Are Love," and "We Are Extensions of Ourselves."

We know we've spoken fast here. We've confused a few of you, we know. But think of it this way: You can always reread this book, read every word carefully, over and over again, until you get it all right. But is there a right? Is there a wrong? Is there a good, a bad, an up, a down? No, dear friends. There is only love. You, that which you perceive, you make right and wrong, good and bad. But in truth, there's no difference. There's only love.

Judgment reduces love, breaks it apart, stops the flow, the ebb. So most people like judgment because they don't like to be in the flow and the ebb. After all, if they were in the flow and the ebb, they certainly wouldn't plunk themselves down on the highway at five o'clock in the morning. Being among individuals with long faces, shaggy beards, undone make-up, bleary-eyed–that is more suitable to their perception of their existence than seeing themselves as love.

But every statement we've given you, no matter how you describe it, regardless of how you observe it, how you interact with it, will lead you back to one thing, just one. Not ten million things! Just one. That one thing is *you.* That one thing is the *I.* Whether you view it from I to you, to we, they, he, she, it–however you choose to describe it–it still comes back to you, dear friends, to yourselves.

Therefore, begin to observe your existence using the defining statements we've given you, and you will observe the amazingness of that which you are, the brilliance of that which you are. You see yourselves as limited beings, dear friends. That is the biggest joke of the universe. For in truth, you are not limited. You are limitless. You are so limitless that you try to put limits on your limitlessness.

You say to yourselves, "I'm a little bit beautiful"; "I'm a little bit amazing"; "I'm a little bit limitless." "Yes, I can do this. I can do that. But I'm not there yet; I'm not perfect. I can't do this; I can't do that. I'm a good hockey player; I'm a good tennis player, but I'm not a very good mathematician or accountant." "I'm a good mother, but I'm not a very good wife." "I'm a good wife, but I'm not a very good mother." "I'm a good worker, but I'm not a very good supervisor or boss." There's always a but, there's always a limit, there's always a reduction. Why—because you don't like seeing yourselves as limitless?

Dear friends, why not see yourselves as the bright, shining individuals that you are? We assure you, this is very fearful for many individuals. They don't want to see their brilliance, their amazingness. For if they do, it means they must do something about it—which is why many individuals will not listen to these six defining statements. Some will listen and set them aside. Some will listen and really learn, and some will never even pick them up.

Why? Because to pick them up means that they would have to begin observing themselves and appreciating their amazingness, their brilliance. And they can't do that yet. They're not willing. Better to place themselves in hot little boxes, with four rubber wheels on it, doing the same repetitive thing five days a week, in a rush. That is the rush of their life. To see themselves being able to get out of work at 4:55 P.M. instead of five o'clock. That's the whole rush of their day.

How many individuals (we assure you, there are quite a few) spend their whole eight hours a day at work waiting for the last five minutes so that they can leave early because then they've done one to the company? They got one over on somebody. Ha! Ha! They left five minutes early, and nobody caught them. And they beat the traffic—and this is the whole thing—they beat the traffic. We hope they beat it senseless.

"Down boy. Don't go there, don't move there, don't cut in front of me. Don't do this, don't do that. Hey you, what are you doing beside me? Don't run so fast; don't drive so fast. Why are you cutting me off like that?" And they do this day in and day out. And they love it. Then they get home, and they say to their spouses, "Do you know what that individual did? Do you know what happened today? Do you know how bad of a day I had? Do you know what's going on? Do you know how frustrated I am? Do you know?" And the poor spouse is sitting there saying, "Do you know, do you know, do you know?" "No, I don't know. Tell me, please. Vent your frustration, I'm a willing receiver. I'm a good sponge, let it out. Give it to me, quick." It lends a whole new meaning to coming home and having a quickie. "Give it to me quick," because the kids are in the kitchen, waiting for you to have supper.

And then wait, because "I've had a bad day, now it's your time to listen." And you do this, and you think you're having a good time. Your life is grand. Everything is as it should be. This is the way it was designed. God created life to be mean, and you're just learning to enjoy it. You're having a good time with it as best as you can.

We assure you, dear friends, if this is the psychology you live in–and we assure you, for the majority of you, it is–then please take a moment, take a deep breath and give yourselves permission to reflect on these six defining statements. They will change your life so much that in less than six months, we assure you, you'll be wondering why you're sitting in traffic doing the same old thing, day in and day out. You will begin making choices that will change your life.

Now, if you enjoy the traffic and you enjoy the aggravation, the frustration; if you enjoy the coffee first thing in the morning and last thing at night because that's the only way you can keep your eyes open while you're traveling; if you enjoy the frustration and the rush of life, then, dear friends, don't listen to these statements. For these statements will change you forever. They will alter your existence. They will move you beyond yourselves. And we assure you, at that point, there will be no turning back.

But if you are on a journey of discovery, of expansion, of growth, then listen to these statements over and over and over again. For the more you listen to them, the more you'll observe how insidiously they move through your life and how much you yourselves have not appreciated how much you choose to extend your existence. The more you'll observe how much your existence is an extension of yourselves, and how little you perceive yourselves as love.

Now, we did promise this. It is time for us to extend ourselves. And as we extend ourselves to all of you, recognize the energy of that which we are. Perceive that which you are, and let that which you are meld with that which we are so that your love can become one with ours and ours with yours. For that which we are is but an extension of God/Goddess/The All That Is, as you are an extension of God/Goddess/The All That Is. Give yourselves time to extend, to observe, to feel, to enjoy, to pleasure. And, dear friends, take a deep breath, that you might observe and enjoy the love, the appreciation of ourselves to yourselves and of yourselves to ourselves. And if tears come to your eyes, let there be tears; let there be joy and let there be love; and let there be a reflection of yourself that you can then see how amazing, brilliant and loving you are.

Dear friends, we do thank you. We do appreciate you, and we do extend ourselves to yourselves in love.

And to you all, God's blessing.

Additional Comments

On love as an energy compared to other forms of energy

Magnetic energy and electrical energy are simply manifestations of the greater energy. This is observed not from the energy perspective, but rather from the resultant of the energy perspective. For example, magnetic energy isn't measured from the perspective of the energy itself, but rather from the perspective of how one part is attracted to another part. As a result, scientists can measure the effect of the attraction from one to another. And this is then described as a magnetic energy. They measure the effect; they do not measure the energy. Electrical energy is similar; they can measure the effect. You see a light bulb, therefore you can perceive the effect of the energy. You can perceive the effect of the energy moving turbines, the effect of the energy operating appliances within a household, within cars. You can measure the effect of the energy, but you cannot measure the energy. Scientists have yet to develop a methodology that measures the actual energy. They simply measure the effect of the energy. However, the key is that they can. They can measure the energy, if they choose to.

Now, they have yet to choose to measure love energy. They have yet to even perceive the effect of the energy of love. There is no willingness on the part of the scientific community (and there certainly is no profit in it) to measure the effect of the energy of love. For the energy of love is a noncontrollable energy. Magnetic energy can be controlled. Electrical energy can be controlled. Microwave energy can be controlled. However, love energy cannot be. There is no methodology, no technique, no device created that would allow control of the energy of love. As a result, there's no desire on the part of any aspect of the scientific community to observe the effect of the energy of love. If they were to observe the effect, they would observe how the energy itself moves events; how the energy allows interactions; how the energy creates attractions; how the energy, in effect, permeates every aspect of existence. For the leaf falling off a tree is as much a manifestation of love energy as two individuals greeting each other on the street.

And so it would require such an immense amount of measurement of observation that, at this point, there is no scientific basis for choosing to do so. And there is no machine, computer or device yet invented that is capable of measuring every permeation of love energy. It isn't as easily definable. As a result, there is no willingness on the part of the scientific community to do so. Now, it can be done. It is easily done. In effect, love energy itself is not magnetic energy, it is not electrical energy, but it encompasses both. Therefore, if instead of attempting to measure the energy, they were to attempt to measure the result of the energy, there would be easier clarity.

Love energy has an actual force, an actual power. It moves; it shifts; it alters; it creates. It is the very basis of all of existence. In effect, it is that which gives life to your cells, to your genes, to your DNA structure, to the very breadth of all of existence. But it also gives life to inanimate objects. It is that which encompasses that which you perceive as auras. It is that which encompasses that which you perceive as life energy. It isn't limited, and therefore, it isn't controllable.

On how the energy of prayer compares to love energy

The energy of prayer is part of love energy, but it isn't love energy. In effect, it is an energy of movement.

The energy of prayer is an energy of attempting to move, attempting to shift, attempting to even control, in effect. But it is part of love energy. Love energy encompasses that, but it is much more than that. View it from this perspective: If you could observe every interaction between every aspect of existence–animate, inanimate and otherwise–then you would observe love energy.

On how love energy can be used to create an environment of love in the world

First, we would suggest, create an environment of love around yourself for yourself–start small and work your way up. And we assure you, it won't take long to work your way up. You can, if you observe the effect of love energy, if you perceive yourselves as love energy. Then dear friends, we assure you, that which you are will expand beyond the boundaries of that which you perceive yourselves to be. And as a result, the environment that you're seeking to create will be created.

Use this one as an example. When this one began his journey many years ago with our assistance, he did not observe himself as love energy. He did not perceive himself as such. Through his growth, through his choices, he's begun to observe himself in that direction and to create an environment surrounding himself in which love energy could exist for himself. And so he expanded. In his expansion, Maggie came into his life. Dear Maggie herself, creating that love energy surrounding herself, expanded herself, and so she chose to merge with this one. And so the two have created an environment.

Then all of you, individually and collectively, have chosen to merge with dear Maggie's and this one's love energy. You've created your own energy environment. And so as a result of this, you create a new loving, expansive environment. Now, observe carefully how much you've altered and shifted the reality around you. How many individuals have you spoken to, have you shared your feelings, your thoughts, your journey, your growth with? How many have observed your progress without even conscious-sharing, and as a result, have made choices themselves that have expanded their existence? Each one of those then has also allowed others to observe them. And so it goes, each one observing and expanding beyond themselves.

From that perspective, it could be said that by choosing to view himself as love energy, to a certain degree, this one began a process. Yet, that would feed his ego, and it isn't about ego-feeding here. This is about recognizing that his choice to manifest himself as that which he is expanded that which already existed. And your choice to manifest yourselves as that which you are expanded that which already exists. And so all of you, from one perspective, are love energy.

On shifting our perception of ourselves to love energy for the sake of calming the weather, since the weather is an extension of our thoughts and choices

If you choose to change the weather, you can. But why would you? Isn't there love in a storm? You see, the ego gets caught up with it. The ego judges that a storm is something bad, something not desirable. And as a result, it wants to change it. We would suggest, this isn't about change as much as it is about acceptance and appreciation. This isn't about saying, "This is good, this is bad. This is right, this is wrong. Let's change the wrong and the bad, and make it good and right." Far from it.

It is about appreciation. For the storm is love energy. It can be appreciated. That it has a force, yes. There is a hurricane presently moving up the eastern coast of this particular continent. That, dear friend, is love energy. Now, some would say that that energy occurred because of lack of love energy, and we would suggest that, from one perspective, it could be observed in that fashion. However, if you observe even more, it will be observed that, in truth, this is love energy manifest. For the storm is clearing up a great number of toxins that exist within the planet at this point in time. From that perspective, therefore, there is a great deal of cleansing going on. There is a great deal of love going on. There's a great deal of nurturing going on. The planet is expanding; it's growing. The consciousness of mankind is expanding and growing. Therefore, it's love energy.

And we would suggest that you take it even further. There are mental blockages being shifted, emotional blockages being shifted, physical blockages being shifted. Not all the toxins are chemicals, dear friends. Some are mankind itself, often created by mankind. As a result, the planet needs to shift. This is part of the normal cycle.

Take your skin, for example. How often do you get a zit? When you do, you look at it and say, "Oh, what an ugly zit. Don't want it." We use the word "zit" because this is common knowledge. It's otherwise known as a pimple; it's otherwise known as an eruption of the skin. However, the zit occurred because the skin is ridding itself of toxins. The toxins are released, sent away from the body. The zit could be compared quite effectively to the hurricane that's existing at this point. It's a big zit, and it will erupt. But it is cleansing.

Now, from one perspective, the ego-personality looks at a zit and says, "This is bad. I must use other chemicals to reduce the zit. It's unsightly; it is unacceptable to society. Therefore, let's put another chemical, such as an acne ointment or something like that, on the zit to reduce it, to remove it."

We assure you, this isn't about clearing or removing the zit, it's about recognizing that the toxins are erupting from the skin, and therefore, it is time to cleanse from within. Let the liver do its work, the kidneys, the pancreas, the organs of elimination. Let them all do their work. The skin is part of the organs of elimination.

The same applies to the planet. The planet has its own way of cleansing itself. Earthquakes, volcanoes, hurricanes, typhoons and weather eruptions are all part of the planet's methodology of cleansing itself.

So if you're observing a great deal of what could be considered extreme weather on the planet right now, it's partly because there's a toxic cleanup taking place and also because, as a people, mankind desires to expand itself. And even though there is a desire to expand itself, there is also a desire to hold itself within. As a result, the only way to expand itself is through eruption, through, as you would call it, violent activity. If the choice was from the perspective of expansion without a necessity to reduce, there would be no violence.

Love energy comes from mankind, from the Earth, from the universe and from everything around you. The energy that affects the weather pattern is affected by mankind, by all of existence on the planet: animate, inanimate, the planet itself as well as aspects of what could be described as push-pulls of the universe around it.

View it from this perspective: There is no existence that lives in isolation, regardless of how you define existence. Therefore, there is no effect, there is no creation that is ever created in isolation. Even God/Goddess/The All That Is was not created in isolation.

Interesting comment, isn't it? We were wondering if you would pick up on it.

God/Goddess/The All That Is was created, but created from all that exists; and therefore, it became all that exists. God/Goddess/The All That Is was never created in isolation; therefore, isolation is not that which it is. It is part of that which it is, but a part that exists within the whole. Isolation exists as part of God/Goddess/The All That Is, but is not God/ Goddess/The All That Is. It's a concept that would be difficult for ourselves to explain here further for, in truth, some would say, "Well then, who created God/Goddess/The All That Is?" And it is not who; it is how. And the *how* goes to concepts far beyond that which the mind–which humanity–is prepared to accept.

One final comment, if we may: Humanity is unwilling to perceive itself as part of all of existence. Therefore, why would it perceive God/Goddess/The All That Is as part of all of existence? Humanity needs from within itself to perceive an existence beyond itself. This is part of the human mind's needs. Yet God/Goddess/The All That Is and humanity differ very little. God/Goddess/The All That Is created itself, and as such, created humanity, it could be said, through many permutations and connotations.

Humanity is unwilling to perceive itself as part of all existence in the same way that it is unwilling to perceive the love energy. But the two are linked. They are intertwined, and they form the very fabric of all of existence.

On love energy and auras

Your auras are part of love energy. They manifest themselves in colors because you choose to view them that way. It is the choice of each individual. We assure you, dear friends, auras themselves are not as you perceive them to be. However, because of the perception of that which is limited to the third-dimensional reality existence in which you live, the perception must fit the dimension that you exist in, and therefore, you perceive it in the form that you perceive it.

Most of you choose not to see the energy. All of you can; most choose not to. For if they were to choose to, it would awaken them to the consciousness that "That Which They Are Is That Which I Am, and That Which I Am Is That Which They Are." Do you see? Interesting statement, isn't it? We thought you might like that.

If you chose to observe the love energy that permeates all of existence, then, dear friends, you would see no separation between one and the other. You would see the definition, but no separation. The difficulty here is in interpreting the concept that we're attempting to describe to you.

View it from this perspective: Presently you sit where you sit. This individual sits where she sits, that individual where she sits. You see separation. You perceive distance between you. But if you were to perceive yourselves as love energy, then, dear friends, there would be no separation. There would be a definition. You would see this individual's energy and your energy and that individual's energy all within the whole. But there would be no separation. For "That Which You Are Is That Which They Are, and That Which They Are Is That Which You Are." Therefore, there would be no difference, no separation–just a simple definition. Defined, not separate. Defined. The couch would be the same energy, but it would have a definition that would define it. And therefore, the definition could be perceived as separation. But once you perceive the separation, then you don't perceive the energy.

In other words, this portion of the energy is you, that portion of the energy is that individual and this portion of the energy is this individual–and let's not forget this other one and that other one either, for they're part of it too. And then dear Maggie, then this one, then ourselves and then there's a few other million individuals surrounding you. But it would all be one.

On love energy and the Radiance Technique®

The Radiance Technique® *is* the love energy. (We did not say it is part of.) Interesting, isn't it? There will be a session on the Radiance Technique®, and we assure you, it will blow your mind. Recognize that that which you see as radiance is, in truth, simply a redirection of love energy. That you use a technique, a methodology, is to your credit. It's not necessary however. Simply to allow yourselves to be the love energy would be enough to experience it in every aspect of your existence. As we said, wait for the session, it will blow your mind–and a number of other concepts that you have. We're looking forward to doing this to all of you. But then it's not us doing it to you, it's you choosing to allow this to be done. And we won't blow your concept away; we simply will rattle your cages a little. Or better yet, we'd simply love you enough to show you a different perspective, a new paradigm of existence.

On judgment versus joy

Judgment is a chosen perspective, yes. But it is not a natural consequence of third-dimensional reality. That judgment exists on the first to the twelfth dimension of reality–and is the main focus of those particular realities–is true. Judgment also exists on the thirteenth to the thirty-first, and to the thirty-second dimension of reality of existence, in fact. However, it is not the main focus. It is not the filter through which perspectives are moved.

The choice to use judgment as a filter is based on a limited perspective of awareness. But it is not a natural consequence; it is a choice. We assure you, you can use joy as a filter from the first to the twelfth just as easily as you use judgment. That does not mean that judgment would not exist; it simply means that the focus would be joy. In fact, from one perspective, it could be said that judgment started from the thirty-second on down. But through perspectives, through alterations, through a willingness to perceive a new paradigm, then, dear friends, judgment has, from one perspective, been limited, and yet, from another perspective, not limited. That it is a filter is true. That is simply an observation of that which it is. However, it is not a natural consequence of that. It is a choice.

When judgment is used as a filter within the thirty-second dimension, the purpose is to observe judgment, and also to observe nonjudgment. How can you observe judgment and nonjudgment, if you do not observe judgment? How can you observe joy, if you don't observe judgment, observe it to its completeness, to its fullness?

On hate

Now hate, that's something different. Hate is judgment twisted, altered, shifted. Take judgment, put it in a bowl, add a pinch of this, a pinch of that, twist it around, and you've got hate. Hate is an emotion; judgment is a perspective. Hate is the emotion that is resultant from judgment through an alteration of the perspective of judgment. Judgment upon judgment upon judgment becomes hate. It is an emotion, and as such, it is an energy.

It is not, however, the opposite of love. You perceive it as the opposite of love, for some in your society say that there's a fine line dividing hate and love. We assure you, that's a good saying for those who like to walk the fence. But it isn't of much more value than that. Love–that which you define as love, as being the opposite of hate–is an emotion, and it's an emotion based on appreciation. Most times, that which individuals define as love is an emotion based on very little appreciation and a lot of need. However, we would suggest that, from the greater perspective, it's an emotion based on a certain degree of appreciation, but not a complete wholeness of appreciation. It is a limited perspective of love energy. It is a limited perspective of absolute appreciation of the self. Therefore, it is coupled with need, limited by need. Hate is an emotion, and love is *the* emotion. To a degree, they can be viewed as opposites, for they manifest in different directions. But they are not opposites of each other, not direct opposites.

On self-love and attracting circumstances of the same vibration

You create circumstances of the same vibration. View it from this perspective, in a practical way: If you perceive yourself as love, instead of allowing yourself to move into a minimum-wage job where the boss is berating–he is denigrating, he basically abuses his employees, works them long hours, pays them very little money–you would never even walk into that door. Instead you would create an environment around yourself whereby someone would look at you and say, "You're a very talented computer individual; you're a very talented dentist. Let me create an environment where you can flourish, where you can blossom."

Or you would choose to create it yourself by simply going to somebody else and saying, "I'm a talented dentist; I'm a talented computer individual," or however you wish to describe yourself. "I can do this, I can do that. Would you like to let me do that? May I help you? May I expand your existence? Allow me to manifest myself so completely that I expand your existence as well as mine." And then it becomes a win-win situation for everyone. You would never take that minimum-wage job.

What people sense most is acceptance as opposed to vibration. "That Which You Are Is That Which I Am," defines acceptance, dear friends. It doesn't say "only under certain occasions."

On self-love versus self-sacrifice

Self-sacrifice, in some cases, is viewed as a noble idea. In fact, some people are revered for sacrificing the self. Witness the number of martyrs in the Catholic Church. We assure you, they are revered: self-sacrifice. In fact, take a look at your society. A man jumps on a grenade so that his fellows aren't killed: self-sacrifice. He's made a hero. Too bad he didn't live to enjoy it. A policeman places his life on the line and gets shot. Too bad he didn't enjoy it, but at least he did a good job. A firefighter, the same. Self-sacrifice is part of your existence, part of how you define yourselves.

In fact, individuals define themselves on the basis of how great the sacrifice they can make. Your whole society reveres people who sacrifice themselves. The more you sacrifice yourselves, the bigger the position you have, the bigger the statue of you they'll raise after you're dead. We assure you, take a look around. Everyone for whom they put a statue up has gone through self-sacrifice–Lenin, Stalin, Roosevelt, Napoleon. However you wish to describe them, whether they are conquerors, creators, politicians or lawyers–even them–we assure you, they all go through self-sacrifice. This is what makes a hero. The greater the sacrifice, the greater the hero.

However, the reason this exists in your society is because as a society and as individuals, you are unwilling to love yourselves so completely that you will give to yourselves all that you need. As a result, you've put sacrifice on a pulpit and kept it there for so long that you've made it holy and revered. And as a result, every member of society, every member of the family, is taught this from generation to generation. It's preached from every pulpit of every religion: "Sacrifice yourself." The reason religions exist is because you sacrifice yourselves. "Give ten percent of everything you own to the religions, please. That way we can survive."

Tithing, good sacrifice. Religious freedom, good sacrifice. Political freedom, good sacrifice. You must sacrifice certain freedoms in order to live in a just society. You must sacrifice the freedom to bear arms in order to live in a society that is free of fear. Poppycock! The whole aspect of sacrifice is poppycock! But if you choose to, you can do this.

However, we would suggest to you, dear friends, of greater benefit is to stop sacrificing. Self-flagellation ended in the thirteenth and fourteenth centuries. There's no longer a need to do so. However, we assure you, there are many individuals who still do. They go around beating themselves. Some do it physically, and some do it mentally. Some do it emotionally, and some still do it spiritually. But they do it.

Recognize, dear friends, that sacrifice is an outdated concept. It's served its purpose well. It's kept you in shackles for most of your existence. The choice is yours: You can stay in shackles, or you can break the shackles and move on. The best way to keep a slave is to make sure that sacrifice is raised to the status of holiness, and then the slave will continue to be a slave willingly.

The same applies. We do not suggest in any fashion that anyone sacrifices anything. What we do suggest is to love yourselves so completely that you are filled to overflowing. When you do this, you do not sacrifice.

You give and you give–and you give more to yourselves-and then when there's so much to give, then you give to others.

We would suggest, instead of tithing to the religions, to the churches, why not give to yourselves? And when there is excess, then give to the churches. We assure you that, from one perspective, society would benefit greatly, even better, for churches would be richer and individuals would be richer. We could speak on this for at least another seventeen years.

On the "rush-rush-rush" treadmill that we create

You create because you like it. You strive for it. You define yourselves by it. It's what gives you your sense of purpose. After all, isn't your sense of purpose to be born, to live, to die? Well, once you're born and you're in the middle of living, the only thing left is to die. So, you rush to it.

It defines that which you are. It gives you a sense of definition, a sense of purpose, a sense of placing yourselves and comparing yourselves to your peers. For, let's face it, ten little monkeys sit all in a row. If one decides not to sit on the chair, what will the others do? Will they jump down and not sit on the chair, or will they sit on the chair and laugh at the other monkey? We would suggest that nine little monkeys would all jump down because nobody wants to be left out. All it takes is one, and then everything changes.

The reason that the society is in such a rush is because it is intent on not knowing itself, on not loving itself. The statement was, "All That I Am Is Love; All That You Are Is Love." How can you apply that statement when you are so busy doing, doing, doing, doing? You're busy sacrificing; you're busy doing. You're busy setting yourselves aside; you're busy reducing yourselves; you're busy altering yourselves; you're busy chasing debt. You're busy chasing everything else. You're so busy, you cannot see yourselves as love.

This is what you want; this is what you strive for. It's what you pray for. Take a look at all the prayers. Someone here mentioned prayers earlier and wanted to know whether prayers were love energy. Listen to the prayers carefully.

"Dear God, please give me the big house that I want. Never mind that it'll have a large mortgage, and I'll barely be able to pay for it; I'll have to get two jobs, and I'll have to work all night, and my family won't see me, and my wife won't know me. But dear God, please give me the new house."

"Dear God, all I want is a good man." But when you get the good man, you find out that the good man isn't so good after all. "Dear God, please get rid of this good man."

"Dear God, all I want is children. Please give me children, dear God." And they pray and they pray. And then when they get children, it's "get out of my hair; get out of my life; get out of the car; get out of the room; go play somewhere." But they've prayed for this. They want this.

If you were to listen to every prayer, dear friends, you would realize how silly prayer really is. Individuals pray, in effect, for the very thing that they really don't want. They don't want to love themselves, in effect. So they pray for not wanting to love themselves. So they pray for an existence that manifests this to themselves.

Now, we're not suggesting here that children are unwanted; in fact, many individuals would argue that with ourselves. "Children are wanted; they are desired; they are loved. It's the stress of life." But we would suggest, if the choice is yours to exist, and you want to have children, then love them. Make them a part of your existence. Don't denigrate them; don't reduce them; don't deny them. And don't tell them in this way, that way, this form, that form, this fashion or that fashion, that they are unwanted and unloved. For in effect, you are unloving yourselves–that child part of yourselves.

And the same applies to the house. If you want a house, get a house. But why get it if it's going to put you into such a turmoil that you'll have to work three jobs to pay the mortgage? Is a 2,533 square-foot home with a circular staircase up the center of it and a three-car garage on a 75-foot-wide lot necessary? Absolutely not. But you've been convinced that it is. Your society has newspaper, radio and television advertisements. Your next-door neighbor has a house; you have to get it as big as his. In fact, better yet, "Let's get one a little bit bigger. That way he can look at us instead of us looking at him."

You strive to accomplish what the other has, and you look to everyone else and say, "That guy must really have it. Look at that. He's got a Jaguar in the garage. He's got a Mercedes outside. He's living in this 3,000-square-foot mansion. Boy, he really must have it. He must have a great life."

Place yourself in his shoes. This is a guy on the verge of a heart attack because he's a workaholic. He eats terribly, doesn't nurture his body; his body's collapsing on itself, feeding on itself. His relationships with his family, his wife and his children are just as good as his body is to himself. And you think he's got it made. So what do you do? You try to emulate him, you try to be just like him. So you go out and you look to do the same thing. "Welcome to Heart-Attack City. Those of you who are almost there, move to the left; those of you who have had it already, to the right. And those of you who are in the middle of getting it, please don't fall on the doorway. We don't like to clean up the mess."

Interesting, isn't it? You're afraid to get off the treadmill, because if you do, you won't have the house, you won't have the cars, you won't have the children. You won't have the heart attacks. You won't have the recognition.

Think of it this way. If you choose, spend the next

three days attending funerals. And listen to the priest and the eulogies for the individuals who you go and visit. Listen to them carefully.

"Here lies Joe. He was a good man. He worked all of his life. Worked two jobs, and unfortunately, he left his poor wife and his three children behind. He left his Mercedes; he left his house; he left his golf clubs. But Joe, we gave you the driver; we left it with you in the coffin, so you can take it with you to heaven. Because we know how much you like to golf. Joe, unfortunately, died young-sixty-eight years old. He had just retired. And here lies Joe, just learning a little golf and he kicks the bucket. What did he die of? Massive coronary. Oh, well. Poor Joe. Hopefully, you bought enough insurance so that your wife and your children are well taken care of."

"Here lies Mary. She was a good wife. She served her husband well. She took care of her children. She always set herself aside. She never ever did anything for herself. She wouldn't even buy herself a dress, virtually walked around the house naked because she didn't have anything to wear. She cooked his meals. She cooked her children's meals. She washed the floor; she cleaned the laundry. She cleaned the dirty underwear. She did this day in and day out. She was such a good wife, such a good mother. Too bad, sixty-three years old, died of cancer. It must have been all those chemicals she was putting her hands in when she was washing the toilet bowls."

We assure you, dear friends, go to the eulogies. You would be surprised. They're all like that. Is this what you want for yourselves? The key, dear friends, is to recognize that this is why you make the choices. Because at the end, when you cast off feet of clay and you're looking down at yourself, you get a eulogy-and you want to make sure you get a good one. So get someone who really knows about you, not just a local priest that they picked up for the ceremony. The key is to recognize that you yourself can, if you choose, enjoy your own eulogy. Or you can choose to alter your existence such that when your eulogy comes along, it's not along those lines.

Realize that this isn't about finding support for your choices. This isn't about looking to others for acceptance. Follow the statements, dear friends. Not one of the statements says, "That which you choose, the others will have to approve." This isn't about the approval of others. Recognize that it is your choice.

The manifestation of your choices may not be very different from your manifestation of your present existence. The key is to recognize that it is your choice, and that you do so out of love. In fact, you can be in an existence and accomplish a great deal. It's just that you do it in a loving way. You do it when the energy is there, when the movement is there, when it flows with you–as opposed to pushing it, forcing it, and moving you in a different direction. The manifestation can take any shape. For ourselves to comment on it further, dear friends, would be to limit your imagination. And far be it for ourselves to limit your imagination.

Glossary Of Terms

cast off feet of clay: the death of an individual.

collective consciousness: the state of consciousness that exists on the eighteenth to the thirty-second dimension of reality.

the conscious mind: that portion of the mind that is conscious of every choice, every action.

dear Maggie: the term used to refer to session director, Maggie McGuffin-Gaudette, Réné's wife.

degrees of benefit: a term to describe the notion that all choice is benefit, but when we judge our choices we assign degrees of benefit.

dimensions of reality: a model of existence in which there are thirty-two dimensions of reality with God/ Goddess/The All That Is residing on the thirty-second dimension. The Wonders reside on the twenty-ninth and humanity resides on the third.

ego-personality: a term used to describe us as individuals; it can be defined as the physical, emotional, mental and manifested spiritual essence.

free choice: the exercise of free will; the action itself.

free will: the ability to choose.

God/Goddess/The All That Is: the essence of oneness of all existence; that which is commonly referred to as God.

group consciousness: the state of consciousness that exists on the twelfth to the eighteenth dimension of reality.

physical, emotional, mental and manifested spiritual: terms used to describe aspects of the self, in terms of the ego-personality; the Wonders use "manifested spiritual" to describe the portion of spirit that we manifest in our lives.

physical senses: the five physical senses that affect ego-personality's physicality: sight, sound, taste, touch and smell.

The Radiance Technique®: a healing technique used to direct love energy. The name of the technique is a registered trademark of the Radiance International. The Wonders have completed a session on this subject entitled "The Radiance Technique®: Pipeline to the Universe".

single or singular consciousness: the state of consciousness that exists on the first to the twelfth dimension of reality; humanity exists on the third dimension of reality, and as such, individuals are viewed as singular consciousnesses.

soul-essence: that which we consider our soul, which

is the extension of God/Goddess/The All That Is on different dimensions of reality.

the subconscious mind: that portion of the mind that is the connection between the conscious mind and soul-essence, and holds all awareness of all existence within it.

this one: the term used to refer to channel Réné Gaudette.

the unconscious mind: that portion of the mind that is unconscious of every choice, every action.

the you that is you: the totality of that which you are; that totality of yourself within yourself, which is the interconnection of soul-essence to ego-personality; this includes our physical, emotional, mental and manifested spiritual essence as well as our conscious, unconscious and subconscious minds.

to your credit: a term used to describe an individual's choice.

How to Contact The Wonders

To find out more about The Wonders or to arrange for a private session, please contact us at the following:

The Wonders, c/o Réné Gaudette
16 Porritt St.
Barrie, Ontario, Canada
L4N 6Y5

Phone: (705) 721-0238
Fax: (705) 721-0598

www.thewonders.com

E-mail
thewonders@thewonders.com

THE ANCIENT SECRET OF THE FLOWER OF LIFE

DRUNVALO MELCHIZEDEK

Drunvalo Melchizedek's life experience reads like an encyclopedia of breakthroughs in human endeavor. He studied physics and art at the University of California at Berkeley, but he feels that his most important education came after college. In the last 25 years, he has studied with over 70 teachers from all belief systems and religious understandings.

For some time now, he has been bringing his vision to the world through the Flower of Life program and the Mer-Ka-Ba meditation. This teaching encompasses every area of human understanding, explores the development of mankind from ancient civilizations to the present time and offers clarity regarding the world's state of consciousness and what is needed for a smooth and easy transition into the 21st century.

VOLUME I

Once, all life in the universe knew the Flower of Life as the creation pattern, the geometrical design leading us into and out of physical existence. Then from a very high state of consciousness, we fell into darkness, the secret hidden for thousands of years, encoded in the cells of all life.

Now we are rising from the darkness and a new dawn is streaming through the windows of perception. This book is one of those windows. Drunvalo Melchizedek presents in text and graphics the Flower of Life Workshop, illuminating the mysteries of how we came to be.

Sacred geometry is the form beneath our being and points to a divine order in our reality. We can follow that order from the invisible atom to the infinite stars, finding ourselves at each step. The information here is one path, but between the lines and drawings lie the feminine gems of intuitive understanding.

SOFTCOVER 228P.

$25.00 ISBN 1-891824-17-1

Chapter Titles:

- **Remembering Our Ancient Past**
- **The Secret of the Flower Unfolds**
- **The Darker Side of Our Present and Past**
- **The Aborted Evolution of Consciousness and the Creation of the Christ Grid**
- **Egypt's Role in the Evolution of Consciousness**
- **The Geometries of the Human Body**
- **The Significance of Shape and Structure**
- **When Evolution Crashed, and the Christ Grid Arose**
- **The Measuring Stick of the Universe: The Human Body and Its Geometries**
- **Reconciling the Fibonacci-Binary Polarity**

Light Technology Published Books

The Flower of Life—Durnvalo Melchizedek

Volume II

The sacred Flower of Life pattern, the primary geometric generator of all physical form, is explored in even more depth in this volume, the second half of the famed Flower of Life workshop. The proportions of the human body, the nuances of human consciousness, the sizes and distances of the stars, planets and moons, even the creations of humankind, are all shown to reflect their origins in this beautiful and divine image. Through an intricate and detailed geometrical mapping, Drunvalo Melchizedek shows how the seemingly simple design of the Flower of Life contains the genesis of our entire third-dimensional existence.

From the pyramids and mysteries of Egypt to the new race of Indigo children, Drunvalo presents the sacred geometries of the Reality and the subtle energies that shape our world. We are led through a divinely inspired labyrinth of science and stories, logic and coincidence, on a path of remembering where we come from and the wonder and magic of who we are.

Finally, for the first time in print, Drunvalo shares the instructions for the Mer-Ka-Ba meditation, step-by-step techniques for the re-creation of the energy field of the evolved human, which is the key to ascension and the next dimensional world. If done from love, this ancient process of breathing prana opens up for us a world of tantalizing possibility in this dimension, from protective powers to the healing of oneself, of others and even of the planet. You may discover a memory or a fleeting reflection of yourself in the following topics:

- ✦ The unfolding of the third informational system
- ✦ Whispers from our ancient heritage
- ✦ Unveiling the Mer-Ka-Ba mediation
- ✦ Using your Mer-Ka-Ba
- ✦ Connecting to the levels of self
- ✦ Two cosmic experiments
- ✦ What we may expect in the forthcoming dimensional shift

$25.00 **Softcover 228p.**
ISBN 1-891824-21-X

Chapter Titles:

- **Spirit and Sacred Geometry**
- **The Left Eye of Horus Mystery School**
- **Ancient Influences on Our Modern World**
- **The Mer-Ka-Ba, the Human Lightbody**
- **The Mer-Ka-Ba Geometries and Meditation**
- **The Mer-Ka-Ba and the Siddhis**
- **Love and Healing**
- **The Three Levels of the Self**
- **Duality Transcended**
- **The Dimensional Shift**
- **The New Children**

THE EXPLORER RACE SERIES

ZOOSH AND OTHERS THROUGH ROBERT SHAPIRO

Superchannel Robert Shapiro can communicate with any personality anywhere and anywhen. He has been a professional channel for over twenty-five years and channels with an exceptionally clear and profound connection.

The Origin... The Purpose...The Future...of Humanity

If you have ever wondered about who you really are, why you are here as part of humanity on this miraculous planet and what it all means, these books in the Explorer Race series can begin to supply the answers—the answers to these and other questions about the mystery and enigma of physical life on Earth.

These answers come from beings who speak through superchannel Robert Shapiro, beings who range from particle personalities to the Mother of all Beings and the thirteen Ssjooo, from advisors to the Creator of our universe to the generators of precreation energies. The scope, the immensity, the mind-boggling infinitude of these chronicles by beings who live in realms beyond our imagination, will hold you enthralled. Nothing even close to the magnitude of the depth and power of this all-encompassing, expanded picture of reality has ever been published.

This amazing story of the greatest adventure of all time and creation is the story of the Explorer Race, of which humans are a small but important percentage. The Explorer Race is a group of souls whose journeys resulted in incarnations in this loop of time on planet Earth, where, bereft of any memory of our immortal selves and most of our heart energy. We came to learn compassion, to learn to take responsibility for the consequences of our actions and to solve creation's previously unsolvable dilemma of negativity. We humans have found a use for negativity—we use it for lust for life and adventure, curiosity and creativity, for doing the undoable. And in a few years we will go out to the stars with our insatiable drive and ability to respond to change and begin to inspire the benign but stagnant civilizations out there to expand and change and grow, which will eventually result in the change and expansion of all creation.

Once you understand the saga of the Explorer Race and what the success of the Explorer Race Experiment means to the totality of creation, you will be proud to be human and to know that you are a vital component of the greatest story ever told—a continuing drama whose adventure continues far into the future.

The Explorer Race Series—Robert Shapiro

Book 1...
the EXPLORER RACE

You individuals reading this are truly a result of the genetic experiment on Earth. You are beings who uphold the principles of the Explorer Race. The information in this book is designed to show you who you are and give you an evolutionary understanding of your past that will help you now. The key to empowerment in these days is to not know everything about your past, but to know that which will help you now.

Your souls have been here for a while on Earth and have been trained in Earthlike conditions. This education has been designed so that you would have the ability to explore all levels of responsibility—results, effects and consequences—and take on more responsibilities.

Your number one function right now is your status of Creator apprentice, which you have achieved through years and lifetimes of sweat. You are constantly being given responsibilities by the Creator that would normally be things that Creator would do. The responsibility and the destiny of the Explorer Race is not only to explore, but to create. SOFTCOVER 574P.

$25.00 ISBN 0-929385-38-1

Chapter Titles:

THE HISTORY OF THE EXPLORER RACE
- The Genetic Experiment on Earth
- Influences of the Zodiac
- The Heritage from Early Civilizations
- Explorer Race Time Line, Part 1
- Explorer Race Time Line, Part 2
- The Experiment That Failed

GATHERING THE PARTS
- The ET in You: Physical Body
- The ET in You: Emotion and Thought
- The ET in You: Spirit

THE JOY, THE GLORY AND THE CHALLENGE OF SEX
- Emotion Lost: Sexual Addiction in Zeta History
- Sex, Love and Relationships
- Sexual Violence on Earth
- The Third Sex: The Neutral Binding Energy
- The Goddess Energy: The Soul of Creation

ET PERSPECTIVES
- Origin of the Species: A Sirian Perception
- An Andromedan Perspective on the Earth Experiment
- The Perspective of Orion Past on Their Role
- Conversation with a Zeta

BEHIND THE SCENES
- The Order: Its Origin and Resolution
- The White Brotherhood, the Illuminati, the New Dawn and the Shadow Government
- Fulfilling the Creator's Destiny
- The Sirian Inheritors of Third-Dimensional Earth

TODAY AND TOMORROW
- The Explorer Race Is Ready
- Coming of Age in the Fourth Dimension
- The True Purpose of Negative Energy
- The Challenge of Risking Intimacy
- Etheric Gene-Splicing and the Neutral Particle
- Material Mastery and the New Safety
- The Sterilization of Planet Earth

THE LOST PLANETS
- The Tenth Planet: The Gift of Temptation
- The Eleventh Planet: The Undoer, Key to Transformation
- The Twelfth Planet: Return of the Heart Energy

THE HEART OF HUMANKIND
- Moving Beyond the Mind
- Retrieving Heart Energy
- The Creator's Mission and the Function of the Human Race

ROBERT SHAPIRO—THE EXPLORER RACE SERIES

Book 2...
ETs and the EXPLORER RACE

In this book, Robert channels Joopah, a Zeta Reticulan now in the ninth dimension, who continues the story of the great experiment—the Explorer Race—from the perspective of his civilization. The Zetas would have been humanity's future selves had not humanity re-created the past and changed the future.

$14.95 SOFTCOVER 237P.
ISBN 0-929385-79-9

Chapter Titles:

- The Great Experiment: Earth Humanity
- ETs Talk to Contactees
- Becoming One with Your Future Self
- ET Interaction with Humanity
- UFOs and Abductions
- The True Nature of the Grays
- Answering Questions in Las Vegas
- UFO Encounters in Sedona
- Joopah, in Transit, Gives an Overview and Helpful Tools
- We Must Embrace the Zetas
- Roswell, ETs and the Shadow Government
- ETs: Friend or Foe?
- ET Presence within Earth and Human Genetics
- Creating a Benevolent Future
- Bringing the Babies Home

Book 3...ORIGINS and the NEXT 50 YEARS

This volume has so much information about who we are and where we came from—the source of male and female beings, the war of the sexes, the beginning of the linear mind, feelings, the origin of souls—it is a treasure trove. Then in addition there is a section that relates to our near future—how the rise of global corporations and politics affects our future, how to use benevolent magic as a force of creation and then how we will go out to the stars and affect other civilizations. Astounding information.

$14.95 SOFTCOVER 339P.
ISBN 0-929385-95-0

Chapter Titles:

THE ORIGINS OF EARTH RACES
- Our Creator and Its Creation
- The White Race and the Andromedan Linear Mind
- The Asian Race, the Keepers of Zeta Vertical Thought
- The African Race and Its Sirius/Orion Heritage
- The Fairy Race and the Native Peoples of the North
- The Australian Aborigines, Advisors of the Sirius System
- The Return of the Lost Tribe of Israel
- The Body of the Child, a Pleiadian Heritage
- Creating Sexual Balance for Growth
- The Origin of Souls

THE NEXT 50 YEARS
- The New Corporate Model
- The Practice of Feeling
- Benevolent Magic
- Future Politics
- A Visit to the Creator of All Creators
- Approaching the One

APPENDIX
- The Body of Man/The Body of Woman

ORIGINS OF THE CREATOR
- Beginning This Creation
- Creating with Core Resonances
- Jesus, the Master Teacher
- Recent Events in Explorer Race History
- The Origin of Creator
- On Zoosh, Creator and the Explorer Race
- Fundamentals of Applied 3D Creationism

Light Technology Published Books

THE EXPLORER RACE SERIES—ROBERT SHAPIRO

Book 4...

CREATORS and FRIENDS
The Mechanics of Creation

Now that you have a greater understanding of who you are in the larger sense, it is necessary to remind you of where you came from, the true magnificence of your being, to have some of your true peers talk to you. You must understand that you are creators in training, and yet you were once a portion of Creator. One could certainly say, without being magnanimous, that you are still a portion of Creator, yet you are training for the individual responsibility of being a creator, to give your Creator a coffee break.

This book will give you peer consultation. It will allow you to understand the vaster qualities and help you remember the nature of the desires that drive any creator, the responsibilities to which that creator must answer, the reaction any creator must have to consequences and the ultimate reward of any creator. This book will help you appreciate all of the above and more. I hope you will enjoy it and understand that maybe more will follow. SOFTCOVER 435P.

\$19.95 ISBN 0-891824-01-5

Chapter Titles:

- **Andastinn, Prototype of Insect Beings**
- **Kazant, a Timekeeper**
- **Founders of Sirius, Creators of Humanoid Forms**
- **A Teacher of Buddha and Time Master's Assistant**
- **Designers of Human Physiology**
- **Avatar of Sea Creatures; and Quatsika, Messenger for the Dimension Makers**
- **The Empath Creator of Seventeen Planets**
- **Shapemaker of Portals**
- **Creator of the Inverse Universe, Our Creator's Creator**
- **Creator of the Void, Preamble to Individuality**
- **The Tornado-Shaped Creator of Creators**
- **The Center of Creation**
- **The Heart Council**
- **Creators of Gold Light and White Light**
- **Creator Talks About Itself and the Explorer Race**
- **Creator Talks About Friends**
- **Creator Speaks of the Stuff of Creation**
- **Creator Discusses Successes and the Outworking of Negativity**
- **Synchronizer of Physical Reality and Dimensions**
- **Master of Maybe**
- **Master of Frequencies and Octaves**
- **Spirit of Youthful Exuberance**
- **Master of Imagination**
- **Zoosh, the End-Time Historian**
- **Master of Feeling**
- **Master of Plasmic Energy**
- **Master of Discomfort Speaks of Himself and the Explorer Race**
- **Master of Discomfort Discusses Light Transference**

Appendix: The Lucifer Gene

Robert Shapiro—The Explorer Race Series

Book 5...
PARTICLE PERSONALITIES

All around you are the most magical and mystical beings. They are too small for you to see as single individuals, but in groups you know them as the physical matter of your daily life. These particles remember where they have been and what they have done in their long lives. We hear from some of them in this extraordinary book. SOFTCOVER 237P.

$14.95 ISBN 0-929385-97-7

Chapter Titles:

- A Particle of Gold
- The Model Maker: The Clerk
- The Clerk; a Mountain Lion Particle; a Particle of Liquid Light; and an Ice Particle
- A Particle of Rose Quartz from a Floating Crystal City
- A Particle of Uranium, Earth's Mind
- A Particle of the Great Pyramid's Capstone
- A Particle of the Dimensional Boundary between Orbs
- A Particle of Healing Energy
- A Particle of Courage Circulating through Earth
- A Particle of the Sun
- A Particle of Ninth-Dimensional Fire
- A Particle of Union
- A Particle of the Gold Lightbeing beyond the Orbs
- A Particle of the Tenfold Wizard
- A Particle of This Creator

Book 6...
EXPLORER RACE and BEYOND

With a better idea of how creation works, we go back to the Creator's advisors and receive deeper and more profound explanations of the roots of the Explorer Race. The liquid domain and the Double Diamond portal share lessons given to the roots on their way to meet the Creator of this universe and finally the roots speak of their origins and their incomprehensibly long journey here. SOFTCOVER 360P.

$14.95 ISBN 1-891824-06-6

Chapter Titles:

- Creator of Pure Feelings and Thoughts, One Circle of Creation
- The Liquid Domain
- The Double-Diamond Portal
- About the Other 93% of the Explorer Race
- Synchronizer of Physical Reality and Dimensions
- The Master of Maybe
- Master of Frequencies and Octaves
- Spirit of Youthful Enthusiasm (Junior) and Master of Imagination
- Zoosh
- The Master of Feeling
- The Master of Plasmic Energy
- The Master of Discomfort
- The Story-Gathering Root Being from the Library of Light/Knowledge
- The Root Who Fragmented from a Living Temple
- The First Root Returns
- Root Three, Companion of the Second Root
- The Temple of Knowledge & the Giver of Inspiration
- The Voice Historian, Who Provided the First Root
- Creator of All That Is

THE EXPLORER RACE SERIES—ROBERT SHAPIRO

Book 7...EXPLORER RACE: the COUNCIL of CREATORS

The thirteenth core members of the Council of Creators discuss their adventures in coming to awareness of themselves and their journeys on the way to the Council on this level. They discuss the advice and oversight they offer to all creators, including the creator of this local universe. These beings are wise, witty and joyous, and their stories of Love's Creation creates an expansion of our concepts as we realize that we live in an expanded, multiple-level reality.

SOFTCOVER 237P.

$14.95 ISBN 1-891824-13-9

Chapter Titles:

- Specialist in Colors, Sounds and Consequences of Actions
- Specialist in Membranes that Separate and Auditory Mechanics
- Specialist in Sound Duration
- Explanation from Unknown Member of Council
- Specialist in Spatial Reference
- Specialist in Gaps and Spaces
- Specialist in Divine Intervention
- Specialist in Synchronicity and Timing
- Specialist in Hope
- Specialist in Honor
- Specialist in Variety
- Specialist in Mystical Connection between Animals and Humans
- Specialist in Change
- Specialist in the Present Moment
- Council Spokesperson and Specialist in Auxiliary Life Forms

Book 8...EXPLORER RACE and ISIS

This is an amazing book. It has priestess training, Shamanic training, Isis adventures with Explorer Race beings—before Earth and on Earth—and an incredibly expanded explanation of the dynamics of the Explorer Race. Isis is the prototypal loving, nurturing, guiding feminine being, the focus of feminine energy. She has the ability to expand limited thinking without making people with limited beliefs feel uncomfortable. She is a fantastic storyteller and all of her stories are teaching stories. If you care about who you are, why you are here, where you are going and what life is all about—pick up this book. You won't lay it down until you are through, and then you will want more. SOFTCOVER 317P.

$14.95 ISBN 1-891824-11-2

Chapter Titles:

- The Biography of Isis
- The Adventurer
- Soul Colors and Shapes
- Creation Mechanics
- Creation Mechanics and Personal Anecdotes
- The Insects' Form and Fairies
- Orion and Application to Earth
- Goddess Section
- Who Is Isis?
- Priestess/Feminine Mysteries

Book 11...EXPLORER RACE: ET VISITORS to EARTH SPEAK

Even as you are searching the sky for extraterrestrials and their space ships, ETs are here on planet Earth—they are stranded, visiting, exploring, studying the culture, healing the Earth of trauma brought on by irresponsible mining or researching the history of Christianity over the last 2000 years. Some are in human guise, some are in spirit form, some look like what we call animals as they come from the species' home planet and interact with those of their fellow beings that we have labeled cats or cows or elephants. Some are brilliant cosmic mathematicians with a sense of humor presently living here as penguins; some are fledgling diplomats training for future postings on Earth when we have ET embassies here. In this book, these fascinating beings share their thoughts, origins and purposes for being here.

$14.95 ISBN 1-891824-28-7

Chapter Titles:

- Stranded Sirian Lightbeing Observes Earth for 800 Years
- An Orion Being Talks about Life on Earth as a Human
- Sensient Redwood
- Quah Earth Religion Researcher
- Visitor to Earth Talks about Pope Pius XII
- Observer Helps Cats Accomplish Their Purpose: Initiating
- A Warrior of Light, the Ultimate Ally
- Penguins: Humorous Mathematicians
- Xri from the Ninth Dimension
- Nurturing the Birth Cord
- Sixth Dimensional Cha-Cha Dances with Humans
- Starlight for Regeneration of Earth's Crystal Veins
- Starlight for Regeneration of Earth's Crystal Veins
- ET Resource Specialists Map and Heal Planetary Bodies
- The Creation and Preparation of the Resource Specialists' Ships Part 3
- Future Zeta Diplomat Learns to Communicate with Humans
- Warrior of Light
- Sirius Water-Being—A Bridge between ETs and Humans
- The Rock-Being Here to Experience Movement
- We Need Benevolent Alien Implants to Go to the Stars
- Ketchin-sa—ET in Dog Form
- Balanced Beings Attempt to Remove Earth Beings' Discomfort

Robert Shapiro—The Explorer Race Series

Book 12...EXPLORER RACE: The HEART is the DOOR to the FUTURE

The opportunity to change the way you live is not only close at hand, it is with you right now. Some of you have felt a change in the air, as you say, the winds of change. And other times it is ephemeral, hard to grasp. It is the ephemeral quality that can help you to know that the good thing that is out of your reach has to do with the future time line. The future time line is also an experience line. It is a sensation line. It is associated with the way your physical body communicates to you and others. It is a way of increasing your sensitivity to your own needs and the needs of others in a completely safe and protected way so that you can respond more quickly and accurately to those needs and appreciate the quality of life around you, much of which you miss because the old time line discourages you from observing. It encourages you to study and understand, but it discourages you from feeling. And it is feeling that is the ultimate answer to your discomforts as well as the pathway to true benevolent insight and fulfillment.

$14.95 ISBN 1-891824-26-0

Chapter Titles:

- Zero Four
- Time Traveler
- Fluid of Time
- Ordinator of Souls
- Energy Three
- Mother of All Beings

Book 13...EXPLORER RACE: THE ULTIMATE UFO BOOK

This is a UFO book with a twist. The beings who channeled through Robert are the ET beings who were on the ships with humans in the famous case files—Betty and Barney Hill, Betty Andreasson, Travis Walton and many, many others. Here is a completely different perspective on the reality of off-planet/Earth-human interactions. As the various beings describe who they are, your understanding of our neighbors in space will expand.

$14.95 ISBN 1-891824-19-8

Chapter Titles:

- ET Contacts
- Daughter of Isis
- Zeta Coordinator
- People of Zeta
- Roswell
- The True Purpose of the Zetas
- Andromedan Diplomatic Liaison to the Zetas and the Parent Race
- Parent Race of Zeta ET Contacts
- Faces of the Visitors
- Visitors' Book & Sirian Mapper
- Bears, Meditation Beings
- Criminals, the Vega Star System and Microbes
- Botucatu, Brazil: Joao and the Andromedans
- Pascagoula, Mississippi: Hickson and Parker
- Guardians at Pascagoula
- The Andromedans: A Tale of a Minister
- Andromedans in Mexico and Professor Hernandez

SHAMANIC SECRETS—ROBERT SHAPIRO

SPEAKS OF MANY TRUTHS AND ZOOSH THROUGH ROBERT SHAPIRO

SHAMANIC SECRETS for MATERIAL MASTERY

Learn to communicate with the planet

This book explores the heart and soul connection between humans and Mother Earth. Through that intimacy, miracles of healing and expanded awareness can flourish.

To heal the planet and be healed as well, we can lovingly extend our energy selves out to the mountains and rivers and intimately bond with the Earth. Gestures and vision can activate our hearts to return us to a healthy, caring relationship with the land we live on.

The character and essence of some of Earth's most powerful features is explored and understood, with exercises given to connect us with those places. As we project our love and healing energy there, we help the Earth to heal from man's destruction of the planet and its atmosphere. Dozens of photographs, maps and drawings assist the process in 25 chapters, which cover the Earth's more critical locations.

$19.95 SOFTCOVER 498P.
ISBN 1-891824-12-0

Chapter Titles:

- **Approaching Material Mastery through Your Physicality**
- **Three Rivers: The Rhine, the Amazon and the Rio Grande**
- **Three Lakes: Pyramid Lake, Lake Titicaca and Lake Baikal**
- **Mountains: Earth's Antennas, Related to the Human Bone Structure**
- **Three Mountains: The Cydonia Pyramid, Mount Rushmore and Mount Aspen**
- **Mountains in Turkey, Japan and California**
- **Eurasia and Man's Skeletal Structure**
- **Greenland, the Land of Mystery**
- **Africa and North America**
- **South and Central America and Australia**
- **Shamanic Interaction with Natural Life**
- **Africa and the Caspian and Black Seas**
- **Mauna Loa, Mount McKinley and Shiprock**
- **The Gobi Desert**
- **Old Faithful, Cayman Islands, Blue Mountains and Grandfather Mountain**
- **Meteor Crater, Angel Falls and Other Unique Locations on the Planet**

PART II, THE FOUNDATION OF ONENESS

- **The Explorer Race as a Part of Mother Earth's Body**
- **Spiritual Beings in a Physical World**
- **Earth Now Releasing Human Resistance to Physical Life**
- **Healing Prisoners, Teaching Students**
- **The Shaman's Key: Feeling and the Five Senses**
- **How to Walk, How To Eat**
- **Breathing: Something Natural We Overlook**
- **How to Ask and Let Go, and How to Sleep**
- **Singing Our Songs**
- **Some Final Thoughts**

SHAMANIC SECRETS for PHYSICAL MASTERY

The purpose of this book is to allow you to understand the sacred nature of your own physical body and some of the magnificent gifts it offers you. When you work with your physical body in these new ways, you will discover not only its sacredness, but how it is compatible with Mother Earth, the animals, the plants, even the nearby planets, all of which you now recognize as being sacred in nature. It is important to feel the value of oneself physically before one can have any lasting physical impact on the world. The less you think of yourself physically, the less likely your physical impact on the world will be sustained by Mother Earth. If a physical energy does not feel good about itself, it will usually be resolved; other physical or spiritual energies will dissolve it because it is unnatural. The better you feel about your physical self when you do the work in the previous book as well as this one and the one to follow, the greater and more lasting will be the benevolent effect on your life, on the lives of those around you and ultimately on your planet and universe. SOFTCOVER 600P.

$19.95 ISBN 1-891824-29-5

Chapter Titles:

- Cellular Clearing of Traumas, Unresolved Events
- Cellular Memory
- Identifying Your Body's Fear Message
- The Heart Heat Exercise
- Learn Hand Gestures
  - —Remove Self-Doubt
  - —Release Pain or Hate
  - —Clear the Adrenals or Kidneys
  - —Resolve Sexual Dysfunction
- Learning the Card Technique for Clarifying Body Message
- Seeing Life as a Gift
- Relationship of the Soul to Personality
- The New Generation of Children
- The Creator and Religions
- Food, Love & Addictions
- Communication of the Heart
- Dreams & Their Significance
- The Living Prayer/Good Life
- Life Force and Life Purpose
- Physical Mastery
- His Life/Mandate for His Ancestors/ Importance of Animals/Emissaries
- Physical Mastery
- Talking to Rain/Bear Claw Story
- Disentanglement
- Grief Culture
- Closing Comments

Dr. Joshua David Stone's Easy to Read

Encyclopedia of the Spiritual Path

$14.95 EACH

THE COMPLETE ASCENSION MANUAL — HOW TO ACHIEVE ASCENSION IN THIS LIFETIME

A synthesis of the past and guidance for ascension. An extraordinary compendium of practical techniques and spiritual history. Compiled from research and channeled information.

ISBN 0-929385-55-1

SOUL PSYCHOLOGY — KEYS TO ASCENSION

Modern psychology deals exclusively with personality, ignoring the dimensions of spirit and soul. this book provides ground-breaking theories and techniques for healing and self-realization.

ISBN 0-929385-56-X

BEYOND ASCENSION — HOW TO COMPLETE THE SEVEN LEVELS OF INITIATION

Brings forth new channeled material that demystifies the 7 levels of initiation and how to attain them. It contains new information on how to open and anchor our 36 chakras.

ISBN 0-929385-73-X

HIDDEN MYSTERIES — AN OVERVIEW OF HISTORY'S SECRETS FROM MYSTERY SCHOOLS TO ET CONTACTS

Explores the unknown and suppressed aspects of Earth's past; reveals new information on the ET movement and secret teachings of the ancient Master schools.

ISBN 0-929385-57-8

THE ASCENDED MASTERS LIGHT THE WAY — KEYS TO SPIRITUAL MASTERY FROM THOSE WHO ACHIEVED IT

Lives and teachings of 40 of the world's greatest saints and spiritual beacons provide a blueprint for total self-realization. Guidance from masters.

ISBN 0-929385-58-6

COSMIC ASCENSION — YOUR COSMIC MAP HOME

Almost all the books on the planet on the subject of ascension are written about planetary ascension. Now, because of the extraordinary times in which we live, cosmic ascension is available here on Earth! Learn about Self-Realization, Evolvement of Nations and more.

ISBN 0-929385-99-3

A BEGINNER'S GUIDE TO THE PATH OF ASCENSION
This volume covers the basics of ascension clearly and completely, from the spiritual hierarchy to the angels and star beings.
ISBN 1-891824-02-3

YOUR ASCENSION MISSION — EMBRACING YOUR PUZZLE PIECE
This book shows how each person's puzzle piece is just as vital and necessary as any other. All aspects of living the fullest expression of your individuality.
ISBN 1-891824-09-0

GOLDEN KEYS TO ASCENSION AND HEALING — REVELATIONS OF SAI BABA AND THE ASCENDED MASTERS
This book represents the wisdom of the ascended masters condensed into concise keys that serve as a spiritual guide. These 420 golden keys present the multitude of insights Dr. Stone has gleaned from his own background and his path to God realization.
ISBN 1-891824-03-1

REVELATIONS OF A MELCHIZEDEK INITIATE
Dr. Stone's spiritual autobiography, beginning with his ascension initiation and progression into the 12th initiation. Filled with insight, tools and information.
ISBN 1-891824-10-4

MANUAL FOR PLANETARY LEADERSHIP
Here at last is an indispensible book that has been urgently needed in these uncertain times. It lays out the guidelines for leadership in the world and in one's life. It serves as a reference manual for moral and spiritual living.
ISBN 1-891824-05-8

HOW TO TEACH ASCENSION CLASSES
This book serves as an ideal foundation for teaching ascension classes and presenting workshops. It covers an entire one- to two-year program of classes.
ISBN 1-891824-15-5

$14.95 EACH

ASCENSION AND ROMANTIC RELATIONSHIPS
Inspired by Djwhal Khul, Dr. Stone has written a unique book about relationships from the perspective of the soul and monad rather than just the personality. This presents a broader picture of the problems and common traps of romantic relationships and offers much deeper advice.
ISBN 1-891824-16-3